Susan Jeffers Ph.D. is an internationally renowned author who has helped millions of people overcome their fears and heal the pain in their lives. She is also a public speaker, workshop leader and media personality who specializes in the areas of personal growth and relationships. She lives with her husband in Los Angeles.

FEEL THE FEAR POWER PLANNER

90 DAYS TO A FULLER LIFE

SUSAN JEFFERS

VERMILION
LONDON

1 3 5 7 9 10 8 6 4 2

Published in 2001 by Vermilion,
an imprint of Ebury Press, Random House,
20 Vauxhall Bridge Road, London SW1V 2SA
www.randomhouse.co.uk

Random House Australia (Pty) Limited
20 Alfred Street, Milsons Point, Sydney,
New South Wales 2061, Australia

Random House New Zealand Limited
18 Poland Road, Glenfield,
Auckland 10, New Zealand

Random House South Africa (Pty) Limited
Endulini, 5A Jubilee Road,
Parktown 2193, South Africa

The Random House Group Limited Reg. No. 954009

Printed and bound in Great Britain by Clays Ltd, St Ives PLC

A CIP catalogue record for this book
is available from the British Library

ISBN 0-7126-0568-1

The Random House Group Limited supports The Forest Stewardship
Council (FSC®), the leading international forest certification organisation.
Our books carrying the FSC label are printed on FSC® certified paper
FSC is the only forest certification scheme endorsed by the leading
environmental organisations, including Greenpeace. Our
paper procurement policy can be found at
www.randomhouse.co.uk/environment

As if I asked a common alms,
And in my wandering hand,
A stranger pressed a Kingdom,
And I, bewildered, stand.

Emily Dickinson

INTRODUCTION

'm very excited to be able to bring to you this life-enhancing Power Planner. You will find that it is very different from other planners, which merely schedule daily appointments. The Power Planner has the added advantage of helping you to connect with the huge amount of power and love you hold inside. As importantly, it is designed to help you focus on the incredible richness in your life.

Your Power Planner puts to work daily many of the tools explained and demonstrated in *Feel the Fear ... and Beyond*. So many people are aware of what they need to do to improve the quality of their lives ... but they don't do it. Why? Because it all seems so overwhelming. Here in a very simple way, I've given you the tools to begin the process. I trust that as you put your Power Planner into daily use, you will soon begin to sense a very deep positive change in the way you are experiencing yourself and the world around you.

Before you begin, here are some helpful suggestions:

1. You will notice that each week begins with a new Statement of Intention that focuses on a different aspect of a beautiful life. It is important that you repeat this Statement of Intention every single day so that its message seeps into the depth of your being. Read it CONSCIOUSLY, focusing on the inherent meaning of each thought, with the ultimate

goal of actually memorizing it by the end of the week. The Statement of Intention will certainly set a wonderfully positive tone for all you do each and every day.

2. I've provided you with daily affirmations. As I am using the term, an affirmation is a strong positive statement that touches the Highest part of who you are. I have found the use of affirmations to be a very effective tool to lessen the negativity of the mind. The good news is that you don't have to believe affirmations for them to work. Just the saying of the positive words has a wonderful effect on your body and your mind.

I suggest you repeat the daily affirmation over and over again (at least ten times in a row) throughout the day while driving your car, while cooking dinner, while feeling stressed at your job, and so on. Remember that the purpose of affirmations is to replace the negativity of the mind with powerful and loving thoughts. This requires repetition, repetition, repetition. You might want to write your daily affirmation on index cards and place them wherever you can see them.

3. On each calendar page, I have included ten sections that represent the Grid of Life. As many of you know from my earlier books, the Grid of Life represents the ingredients of a rich and meaningful life. When your life is rich and meaningful in many areas – family, friends, career, relationship, contribution to community, personal growth and whatever else you want to put into it – you experience a life-enhancing result ... your fear in any one area of your life lessens dramatically. And your confidence grows and grows.

You'll notice I left more room in the area of career. *This is not because career is more important than the rest*, but because the other categories will most likely have fewer items in any given day. (The area of career also includes the tasks of a full-time homemaker which, after all, is a career in its own right.)

'The Dynamic Duo' at the top of each page is there to remind you that in each area of your Grid of Life, you are truly important. Too many of us don't realize how important we are to the people around us. How empowering it is to understand that we truly do have meaning and purpose and then let all our actions come from that premise. If you don't have this understanding, simply ask yourself an essential question as you are planning your activities for each day: 'If I were really important, what would I be doing in each area of my life?' And then do it. Begin by filling each of the sections of your Power Planner with actions that you can take that come from that essential question. *As you continue to act-as-if your life has meaning, eventually you will live into this profoundly important understanding.*

4. I've included a 'Risk of the Day' section to help you expand your 'Comfort Zone'. *Remember: These risks should not include physically dangerous acts or any acts that hurt other people.* The risks you are to choose are life-affirming risks. For example a phone call you've been hesitant to make, eating alone in a restaurant for the first time, inviting someone to lunch, taking a step to heal a relationship, going to the doctor and other acts that may make you uncomfortable. Little by little, the world will seem much more manageable as your comfort level grows and grows.

5. I've included a 'Gratitude' section. It is essential that as you go through each day you learn to focus on the 'ordinary miracles' of everyday life – the little things that we too often take for granted: the sunset, a compliment from a friend, finding a parking place, good health, the food we eat and so on. Our noticing of these ordinary miracles makes for a much happier day! Too many of us tend to focus only on the negative … the perfect recipe for doom and gloom.

6. Each day includes a Pain-to-Power chart. Mark a spot where you see yourself that particular day. Naturally, there will be days when you slip backwards a bit, but hopefully, as time goes by, your sense of power and love will increase. If it doesn't, perhaps you are judging yourself too harshly instead of patting yourself on the back for the work you are doing! Remember, patting yourself on the back is a very important part of feeling powerful and loving!

7. There will be times, when you can't focus on all areas of your Personal Planner because of a special project at work, or family considerations, or ill health. Not to worry. These diversions are to be expected. At such times, don't drive yourself crazy lamenting that you are not building a rich and meaningful life! Even if you don't fill in all the boxes in a given day, they will be there as a constant reminder of the beauty in your life. Remember, your goal is to create *an attitude* of fullness and an inner sense of power and love.

8. To give you a greater depth of understanding of each area of your Power Planner, consult my earlier book *Feel the Fear ... And Beyond*. It was in this book that the Power Planner was born and it describes in depth why each area of your Power Planner is so important and how you can use each area more effectively. As you may have already discovered, a periodic refresher of uplifting material helps keep you on the road to a more powerful and loving life.

In the beginning, the use of the Power Planner will require conscious attention. But as you continue to use it, powerful living will become second nature. You will easily and automatically begin to realize the richness and beauty in your life. Remember, LIFE IS HUGE! Enjoy it all!

From my heart to yours,

SAMPLE DAY USING YOUR POWER PLANNER

DAY 1   **DATE** *1/1/01*

Affirmation of the Day
I am powerful and I am loving and I have nothing to fear.

> I commit 100% to each area of my life.
> I know that I count and I act as if I do.

MY LIFE IS RICH!

FAMILY *Call Aunt Alice and make sure she is feeling better.*

FRIENDS *Invite Betty to lunch.*

HEALTH *Exercise for 20 minutes.*

PERSONAL GROWTH *Go to my French class.*

SPIRITUAL GROWTH *Do my affirmations for 20 minutes through-out the day.*

ALONE TIME *Take a long, hot bath.*

RELATIONSHIP *Call my boyfriend and tell him how much I love him.*

CONTRIBUTION TO COMMUNITY *Arrange to send some clothes to the Homeless Shelter.*

PLAYTIME *Meet Carole for a snack after work.*

WORK *Work on the Proposal for the Sacks account, Call Bob Myers to see if he got my package, Come up with a new idea for the Grant account, thank Anne for being such a caring workmate.*

RISK OF THE DAY *Invite my boss for lunch to discuss some of my ideas.*

TODAY I AM GRATEFUL FOR *my health, my car started, the sun is shining, lunch was delicious, the good feeling when I brought in some doughnuts and coffee for the office, my family and friends, my wonderful job ... and my boyfriend.*

Where do I belong today on my Pain-to-Power Chart?

▶ ▶ ▶ ▶ ▶ ▶ ▶ ▶ ▶ ▶ ▶ ▶ ▶ ⊙ ▶ ▶ ▶ ▶ ▶ ▶

PAIN   **POWER**

SO TO BEGIN . . .

am powerful and I am loving and I have nothing to fear I am powerful and
g and I have nothing to fear I am powerful and I am loving and I have nothi
am powerful and I am loving and I have nothing to fear I am powerful and

This week I focus on
COURAGE

and I have nothing to fear I am powerful and I am loving and I have nothi
am powerful and I am loving and I have nothing to fear I am powerful and
g and I have nothing to fear I am powerful and I am loving and I have nothi
am powerful and I am loving and I have nothing to I am powerful and I am l
have nothing to fear I am powerful and I am loving and I have nothing to
owerful and I am loving and I have nothing to fear I am powerful and I am l
have nothing to fear I am powerful and I am loving and I have nothing to
owerful and I am loving and I have nothing to fear I am powerful and I am l
have nothing to fear I am powerful and I am loving and I have nothing to
owerful and I am loving and I have nothing to fear I am powerful and I am l
have nothing to fear I am powerful and I am loving and I have nothing to
owerful and I am loving and I have nothing to fear I am powerful and I am l
have nothing to fear I am powerful and I am loving and I have nothing to
owerful and I am loving and I have nothing to fear I am powerful and I am l
have nothing to fear I am powerful and I am loving and I have nothing to
owerful and I am loving and I have nothing to fear I am powerful and I am l
have nothing to fear I am powerful and I am loving and I have nothing to
owerful and I am loving and I have nothing to fear I am powerful and I am l
have nothing to fear I am powerful and I am loving and I have nothing to
owerful and I am loving and I have nothing to fear I am powerful and I am l
have nothing to fear I am powerful and I am loving and I have nothing to

STATEMENT OF INTENTION

I move into life knowing there is nothing to fear. I push away all self-doubt and replace it with self-trust. Within me is an endless source of wisdom and strength that will handle all that needs to be handled. I see the huge expanse of possibility that lies before me. I constantly remind myself my life is unfolding in a perfect way. I trust the 'Grand Design'. I am being shown the way.

Remember that the Statements of Intention are to be repeated DAILY and hopefully memorized.

Affirmation of the Day

I am powerful and I am loving and I have nothing to fear.

> I commit 100% to each area of my life.
> I know that I count and I act as if I do.

MY LIFE IS RICH!

FAMILY

FRIENDS

HEALTH

PERSONAL GROWTH

SPIRITUAL GROWTH

ALONE TIME

RELATIONSHIP

CONTRIBUTION TO COMMUNITY

PLAYTIME

WORK

RISK OF THE DAY

TODAY I AM GRATEFUL FOR

Where do I belong today on my Pain-to-Power Chart?

▶ ▶

PAIN   **POWER**

STATEMENT OF INTENTION

I move into life knowing there is nothing to fear. I push away all self-doubt and replace it with self-trust. Within me is an endless source of wisdom and strength that will handle all that needs to be handled. I see the huge expanse of possibility that lies before me. I constantly remind myself my life is unfolding in a perfect way. I trust the 'Grand Design'. I am being shown the way.

Affirmation of the Day

I relax knowing that I can handle all that needs to be handled.

> I commit 100% to each area of my life.
> I know that I count and I act as if I do.

MY LIFE IS RICH!

FAMILY

FRIENDS

HEALTH

PERSONAL GROWTH

SPIRITUAL GROWTH

ALONE TIME

RELATIONSHIP

CONTRIBUTION TO COMMUNITY

PLAYTIME

WORK

RISK OF THE DAY

TODAY I AM GRATEFUL FOR

Where do I belong today on my Pain-to-Power Chart?

▶ ▶

PAIN   **POWER**

STATEMENT OF INTENTION

I move into life knowing there is nothing to fear. I push away all self-doubt and replace it with self-trust. Within me is an endless source of wisdom and strength that will handle all that needs to be handled. I see the huge expanse of possibility that lies before me. I constantly remind myself my life is unfolding in a perfect way. I trust the 'Grand Design'. I am being shown the way.

Affirmation of the Day

I am powerful and I love it!

I commit 100% to each area of my life.
I know that I count and I act as if I do.

MY LIFE IS RICH!

FAMILY

FRIENDS

HEALTH

PERSONAL GROWTH

SPIRITUAL GROWTH

ALONE TIME

RELATIONSHIP

CONTRIBUTION TO COMMUNITY

PLAYTIME

WORK

RISK OF THE DAY

TODAY I AM GRATEFUL FOR

Where do I belong today on my Pain-to-Power Chart?

▶ ▶ ▶ ▶ ▶ ▶ ▶ ▶ ▶ ▶ ▶ ▶ ▶ ▶ ▶ ▶ ▶ ▶ ▶ ▶

PAIN   **POWER**

STATEMENT OF INTENTION

I move into life knowing there is nothing to fear. I push away all self-doubt and replace it with self-trust. Within me is an endless source of wisdom and strength that will handle all that needs to be handled. I see the huge expanse of possibility that lies before me. I constantly remind myself my life is unfolding in a perfect way. I trust the 'Grand Design'. I am being shown the way.

Affirmation of the Day

I stand tall and take respnsibility for my life.

> I commit 100% to each area of my life.
> I know that I count and I act as if I do.

MY LIFE IS RICH!

FAMILY

FRIENDS

HEALTH

PERSONAL GROWTH

SPIRITUAL GROWTH

ALONE TIME

RELATIONSHIP

CONTRIBUTION TO COMMUNITY

PLAYTIME

WORK

RISK OF THE DAY

TODAY I AM GRATEFUL FOR

Where do I belong today on my Pain-to-Power Chart?

▶▶▶▶▶▶▶▶▶▶▶▶▶▶▶▶▶▶▶▶▶▶▶

PAIN   POWER

STATEMENT OF INTENTION

I move into life knowing there is nothing to fear. I push away all self-doubt and replace it with self-trust. Within me is an endless source of wisdom and strength that will handle all that needs to be handled. I see the huge expanse of possibility that lies before me. I constantly remind myself my life is unfolding in a perfect way. I trust the 'Grand Design'. I am being shown the way.

Affirmation of the Day

I know I can handle whatever happens in my life.

> I commit 100% to each area of my life.
> I know that I count and I act as if I do.

MY LIFE IS RICH!

FAMILY

FRIENDS

HEALTH

PERSONAL GROWTH

SPIRITUAL GROWTH

ALONE TIME

RELATIONSHIP

CONTRIBUTION TO COMMUNITY

PLAYTIME

WORK

RISK OF THE DAY

TODAY I AM GRATEFUL FOR

Where do I belong today on my Pain-to-Power Chart?

▶ ▶

PAIN   **POWER**

STATEMENT OF INTENTION

I move into life knowing there is nothing to fear. I push away all self-doubt and replace it with self-trust. Within me is an endless source of wisdom and strength that will handle all that needs to be handled. I see the huge expanse of possibility that lies before me. I constantly remind myself my life is unfolding in a perfect way. I trust the 'Grand Design'. I am being shown the way.

Affirmation of the Day

I am moving forward with confidence and love.

> I commit 100% to each area of my life.
> I know that I count and I act as if I do.

MY LIFE IS RICH!

FAMILY

FRIENDS

HEALTH

PERSONAL GROWTH

SPIRITUAL GROWTH

ALONE TIME

RELATIONSHIP

CONTRIBUTION TO COMMUNITY

PLAYTIME

WORK

RISK OF THE DAY

TODAY I AM GRATEFUL FOR

Where do I belong today on my Pain-to-Power Chart?

▶ ▶

PAIN   **POWER**

move into life knowing there is nothing to fear. I push away all self-doubt and replace it with self-trust. Within me is an endless source of wisdom and strength that will handle all that needs to be handled. I see the huge expanse of possibility that lies before me. I constantly remind myself my life is unfolding in a perfect way. I trust the 'Grand Design'. I am being shown the way.

Affirmation of the Day

*I trust that my inner wisdom will lead me to
wherever I need to go.*

I commit 100% to each area of my life.
I know that I count and I act as if I do.

MY LIFE IS RICH!

FAMILY

FRIENDS

HEALTH

PERSONAL GROWTH

SPIRITUAL GROWTH

ALONE TIME

RELATIONSHIP

CONTRIBUTION TO COMMUNITY

PLAYTIME

WORK

RISK OF THE DAY

TODAY I AM GRATEFUL FOR

Where do I belong today on my Pain-to-Power Chart?

▶ ▶

PAIN   **POWER**

This week I focus on

ABUNDANCE

my life is rich my life is rich

STATEMENT OF INTENTION

I am focusing on the 'ordinary miracles' that surround me. I take nothing for granted. There is so much to be grateful for and I notice it all ... a sweet smile, a delicious meal, wonderful friends, a flower, my health, my ability to contribute to this needy world. Yes, my world is abundant and I glow from the riches in my life.

Affirmation of the Day

I am drawing all good things into my life.

> I commit 100% to each area of my life.
> I know that I count and I act as if I do.

MY LIFE IS RICH!

FAMILY

FRIENDS

HEALTH

PERSONAL GROWTH

SPIRITUAL GROWTH

ALONE TIME

RELATIONSHIP

CONTRIBUTION TO COMMUNITY

PLAYTIME

WORK

RISK OF THE DAY

TODAY I AM GRATEFUL FOR

Where do I belong today on my Pain-to-Power Chart?

▶ ▶

PAIN   **POWER**

STATEMENT OF INTENTION

I am focusing on the 'ordinary miracles' that surround me. I take nothing for granted. There is so much to be grateful for and I notice it all ... a sweet smile, a delicious meal, wonderful friends, a flower, my health, my ability to contribute to this needy world. Yes, my world is abundant and I glow from the riches in my life.

Affirmation of the Day

*I have within me enough power and love to create
all that I shall ever need.*

> I commit 100% to each area of my life.
> I know that I count and I act as if I do.

MY LIFE IS RICH!

FAMILY

FRIENDS

HEALTH

PERSONAL GROWTH

SPIRITUAL GROWTH

ALONE TIME

RELATIONSHIP

CONTRIBUTION TO COMMUNITY

PLAYTIME

WORK

RISK OF THE DAY

TODAY I AM GRATEFUL FOR

Where do I belong today on my Pain-to-Power Chart?

▶▶▶▶▶▶▶▶▶▶▶▶▶▶▶▶▶▶▶▶▶▶

PAIN   **POWER**

I am focusing on the 'ordinary miracles' that surround me. I take nothing for granted. There is so much to be grateful for and I notice it all … a sweet smile, a delicious meal, wonderful friends, a flower, my health, my ability to contribute to this needy world. Yes, my world is abundant and I glow from the riches in my life.

Affirmation of the Day

I take time to give thanks for all the blessings in my life.

> I commit 100% to each area of my life.
> I know that I count and I act as if I do.

MY LIFE IS RICH!

FAMILY

FRIENDS

HEALTH

PERSONAL GROWTH

SPIRITUAL GROWTH

ALONE TIME

RELATIONSHIP

CONTRIBUTION TO COMMUNITY

PLAYTIME

WORK

RISK OF THE DAY

TODAY I AM GRATEFUL FOR

Where do I belong today on my Pain-to-Power Chart?

▶ ▶

PAIN   **POWER**

STATEMENT OF INTENTION

I am focusing on the 'ordinary miracles' that surround me. I take nothing for granted. There is so much to be grateful for and I notice it all ... a sweet smile, a delicious meal, wonderful friends, a flower, my health, my ability to contribute to this needy world. Yes, my world is abundant and I glow from the riches in my life.

Affirmation of the Day

Life IS huge and I embrace it all!

> I commit 100% to each area of my life.
> I know that I count and I act as if I do.

MY LIFE IS RICH!

FAMILY

FRIENDS

HEALTH

PERSONAL GROWTH

SPIRITUAL GROWTH

ALONE TIME

RELATIONSHIP

CONTRIBUTION TO COMMUNITY

PLAYTIME

WORK

RISK OF THE DAY

TODAY I AM GRATEFUL FOR

Where do I belong today on my Pain-to-Power Chart?

▶ ▶

PAIN   **POWER**

STATEMENT OF INTENTION

I am focusing on the 'ordinary miracles' that surround me. I take nothing for granted. There is so much to be grateful for and I notice it all ... a sweet smile, a delicious meal, wonderful friends, a flower, my health, my ability to contribute to this needy world. Yes, my world is abundant and I glow from the riches in my life.

Affirmation of the Day

I keep my heart open to receive all the riches before me.

> I commit 100% to each area of my life.
> I know that I count and I act as if I do.

MY LIFE IS RICH!

FAMILY

FRIENDS

HEALTH

PERSONAL GROWTH

SPIRITUAL GROWTH

ALONE TIME

RELATIONSHIP

CONTRIBUTION TO COMMUNITY

PLAYTIME

WORK

RISK OF THE DAY

TODAY I AM GRATEFUL FOR

Where do I belong today on my Pain-to-Power Chart?

▶ ▶

PAIN   **POWER**

STATEMENT OF INTENTION

I am focusing on the 'ordinary miracles' that surround me. I take nothing for granted. There is so much to be grateful for and I notice it all ... a sweet smile, a delicious meal, wonderful friends, a flower, my health, my ability to contribute to this needy world. Yes, my world is abundant and I glow from the riches in my life.

Affirmation of the Day

I smile as I recognize the many blessings in my life.

> I commit 100% to each area of my life.
> I know that I count and I act as if I do.

MY LIFE IS RICH!

FAMILY

FRIENDS

HEALTH

PERSONAL GROWTH

SPIRITUAL GROWTH

ALONE TIME

RELATIONSHIP

CONTRIBUTION TO COMMUNITY

PLAYTIME

WORK

RISK OF THE DAY

TODAY I AM GRATEFUL FOR

Where do I belong today on my Pain-to-Power Chart?

▶ ▶ ▶ ▶ ▶ ▶ ▶ ▶ ▶ ▶ ▶ ▶ ▶ ▶ ▶ ▶ ▶ ▶ ▶ ▶

PAIN   **POWER**

STATEMENT OF INTENTION

I am focusing on the 'ordinary miracles' that surround me. I take nothing for granted. There is so much to be grateful for and I notice it all ... a sweet smile, a delicious meal, wonderful friends, a flower, my health, my ability to contribute to this needy world. Yes, my world is abundant and I glow from the riches in my life.

Affirmation of the Day

I share my abundance with everyone around me.

> I commit 100% to each area of my life.
> I know that I count and I act as if I do.

MY LIFE IS RICH!

FAMILY

FRIENDS

HEALTH

PERSONAL GROWTH

SPIRITUAL GROWTH

ALONE TIME

RELATIONSHIP

CONTRIBUTION TO COMMUNITY

PLAYTIME

WORK

RISK OF THE DAY

TODAY I AM GRATEFUL FOR

Where do I belong today on my Pain-to-Power Chart?

▶ ▶

PAIN   **POWER**

I have much to give I have much to give I have much to give I have much to
e much to give I have much to give I have much to give I have much to give I
to give I have much to give I have much to give I have much to give I have

This week I focus on

CONTRIBUTION

to give I have much to give I have much to give I have much to give I have
e I have much to give I have much to give I have much to give I have much to
e much to give I have much to give I have much to give I have much to give I
to give I have much to give I have much to give I have much to give I have
e I have much to give I have much to give I have much to give I have much to
e much to give I have much to give I have much to give I have much to give I
to give I have much to give I have much to give I have much to give I have
e I have much to give I have much to give I have much to give I have much to
e much to give I have much to give I have much to give I have much to give I
to give I have much to give I have much to give I have much to give I have
e I have much to give I have much to give I have much to give I have much to
e much to give I have much to give I have much to give I have much to give I
to give I have much to give I have much to give I have much to give I have
e I have much to give I have much to give I have much to give I have much to
e much to give I have much to give I have much to give I have much to give I
to give I have much to give I have much to give I have much to give I have
e I have much to give I have much to give I have much to give I have much to
e much to give I have much to give I have much to give I have much to give I

STATEMENT OF INTENTION

I now commit to helping heal the world around me. I have been given so much. Every day, I ask myself, 'How can I be more helpful here?' And I take loving action. I am mindful of those in need and offer a helping hand. In this way, I am touching the best of who I am and sharing it with a very needy world. I know my life has meaning and I am thankful that I have so much to give.

Affirmation of the Day

I joyfully say 'thank you' to all who contribute to my life.

> I commit 100% to each area of my life.
> I know that I count and I act as if I do.

MY LIFE IS RICH!

FAMILY

FRIENDS

HEALTH

PERSONAL GROWTH

SPIRITUAL GROWTH

ALONE TIME

RELATIONSHIP

CONTRIBUTION TO COMMUNITY

PLAYTIME

WORK

RISK OF THE DAY

TODAY I AM GRATEFUL FOR

Where do I belong today on my Pain-to-Power Chart?

▶ ▶

PAIN   **POWER**

STATEMENT OF INTENTION

I now commit to helping heal the world around me. I have been given so much. Every day, I ask myself, 'How can I be more helpful here?' And I take loving action. I am mindful of those in need and offer a helping hand. In this way, I am touching the best of who I am and sharing it with a very needy world. I know my life has meaning and I am thankful that I have so much to give.

Affirmation of the Day

*I commit to participating 100% in the healing of
the world around me.*

I commit 100% to each area of my life.
I know that I count and I act as if I do.

MY LIFE IS RICH!

FAMILY

FRIENDS

HEALTH

PERSONAL GROWTH

SPIRITUAL GROWTH

ALONE TIME

RELATIONSHIP

CONTRIBUTION TO COMMUNITY

PLAYTIME

WORK

RISK OF THE DAY

TODAY I AM GRATEFUL FOR

Where do I belong today on my Pain-to-Power Chart?

▶ ▶

PAIN   **POWER**

STATEMENT OF INTENTION

I now commit to helping heal the world around me. I have been given so much. Every day, I ask myself, 'How can I be more helpful here?' And I take loving action. I am mindful of those in need and offer a helping hand. In this way, I am touching the best of who I am and sharing it with a very needy world. I know my life has meaning and I am thankful that I have so much to give.

Affirmation of the Day

I pick up the mirror and ask 'how can I be more helpful here?'

> I commit 100% to each area of my life.
> I know that I count and I act as if I do.

MY LIFE IS RICH!

FAMILY

FRIENDS

HEALTH

PERSONAL GROWTH

SPIRITUAL GROWTH

ALONE TIME

RELATIONSHIP

CONTRIBUTION TO COMMUNITY

PLAYTIME

WORK

RISK OF THE DAY

TODAY I AM GRATEFUL FOR

Where do I belong today on my Pain-to-Power Chart?

▶ ▶

PAIN   **POWER**

STATEMENT OF INTENTION

now commit to helping heal the world around me. I have been given so much. Every day, I ask myself, 'How can I be more helpful here?' And I take loving action. I am mindful of those in need and offer a helping hand. In this way, I am touching the best of who I am and sharing it with a very needy world. I know my life has meaning and I am thankful that I have so much to give.

Affirmation of the Day

I am creating a better world at home, at work and at play.

> I commit 100% to each area of my life.
> I know that I count and I act as if I do.

MY LIFE IS RICH!

FAMILY

FRIENDS

HEALTH

PERSONAL GROWTH

SPIRITUAL GROWTH

ALONE TIME

RELATIONSHIP

CONTRIBUTION TO COMMUNITY

PLAYTIME

WORK

RISK OF THE DAY

TODAY I AM GRATEFUL FOR

Where do I belong today on my Pain-to-Power Chart?

▶ ▶
PAIN   **POWER**

STATEMENT OF INTENTION

I now commit to helping heal the world around me. I have been given so much. Every day, I ask myself, 'How can I be more helpful here?' And I take loving action. I am mindful of those in need and offer a helping hand. In this way, I am touching the best of who I am and sharing it with a very needy world. I know my life has meaning and I am thankful that I have so much to give.

Affirmation of the Day

My life makes a difference to everyone around me.

I commit 100% to each area of my life.
I know that I count and I act as if I do.

MY LIFE IS RICH!

FAMILY

FRIENDS

HEALTH

PERSONAL GROWTH

SPIRITUAL GROWTH

ALONE TIME

RELATIONSHIP

CONTRIBUTION TO COMMUNITY

PLAYTIME

WORK

RISK OF THE DAY

TODAY I AM GRATEFUL FOR

Where do I belong today on my Pain-to-Power Chart?

▶ ▶
PAIN   **POWER**

STATEMENT OF INTENTION

I now commit to helping heal the world around me. I have been given so much. Every day, I ask myself, 'How can I be more helpful here?' And I take loving action. I am mindful of those in need and offer a helping hand. In this way, I am touching the best of who I am and sharing it with a very needy world. I know my life has meaning and I am thankful that I have so much to give.

Affirmation of the Day

*I rise above my fear and focus on all I have
to give to the world.*

I commit 100% to each area of my life.
I know that I count and I act as if I do.

MY LIFE IS RICH!

FAMILY

FRIENDS

HEALTH

PERSONAL GROWTH

SPIRITUAL GROWTH

ALONE TIME

RELATIONSHIP

CONTRIBUTION TO COMMUNITY

PLAYTIME

WORK

RISK OF THE DAY

TODAY I AM GRATEFUL FOR

Where do I belong today on my Pain-to-Power Chart?

▶ ▶ ▶ ▶ ▶ ▶ ▶ ▶ ▶ ▶ ▶ ▶ ▶ ▶ ▶ ▶ ▶ ▶ ▶ ▶

PAIN   **POWER**

STATEMENT OF INTENTION

I now commit to helping heal the world around me. I have been given so much. Every day, I ask myself, 'How can I be more helpful here?' And I take loving action. I am mindful of those in need and offer a helping hand. In this way, I am touching the best of who I am and sharing it with a very needy world. I know my life has meaning and I am thankful that I have so much to give.

Affirmation of the Day

I'm committed to helping heal the world around me.

> I commit 100% to each area of my life.
> I know that I count and I act as if I do.

MY LIFE IS RICH!

FAMILY

FRIENDS

HEALTH

PERSONAL GROWTH

SPIRITUAL GROWTH

ALONE TIME

RELATIONSHIP

CONTRIBUTION TO COMMUNITY

PLAYTIME

WORK

RISK OF THE DAY

TODAY I AM GRATEFUL FOR

Where do I belong today on my Pain-to-Power Chart?

▶ ▶

PAIN   **POWER**

touch I reach out and I touch I reach out and I touch I reach out and I touch I r
nd I touch I reach out and I touch I reach out and I touch I reach out and I to
out and I touch I reach out and I touch I reach out and I touch I reach out
I re‌ ‌uch I reac
tou‌ ‌reach ou
h I r‌ ‌uch I reac
tou‌ ‌I touch I
nd I‌ ‌t and I tc
out‌ ‌each out
I re‌ ‌uch I reac
tou‌ ‌I touch I

This week I focus on
CONNECTION

nd I touch I reach out and I touch I reach out and I touch I reach out and I to
out and I touch I reach out and I touch I reach out and I touch I reach out
I reach out and I touch I reach out and I touch I reach out and I touch I reac
touch I reach out and I touch I reach out and I touch I reach out and I touch I
nd I touch I reach out and I touch I reach out and I touch I reach out and I to
out and I touch I reach out and I touch I reach out and I touch I reach out
I reach out and I touch I reach out and I touch I reach out and I touch I reac
touch I reach out and I touch I reach out and I touch I reach out and I touch I
nd I touch I reach out and I touch I reach out and I touch I reach out and I t
out and I touch I reach out and I touch I reach out and I touch I reach out
I reach out and I touch I reach out and I touch I reach out and I touch I reac
touch I reach out and I touch I reach out and I touch I reach out and I touch I
and I touch I reach out and I touch I reach out and I touch I reach out and I t
out and I touch I reach out and I touch I reach out and I touch I reach out
I reach out and I touch I reach out and I touch I reach out and I touch I rea
touch I reach out and I touch I reach out and I touch I reach out and I touch I
and I touch I reach out and I touch I reach out and I touch I reach out and I t
out and I touch I reach out and I touch I reach out and I touch I reach out
I reach out and I touch I reach out and I touch I reach out and I touch I rea
touch I reach out and I touch I reach out and I touch I reach out and I touch I
and I touch I reach out and I touch I reach out and I touch I reach out and I t

STATEMENT OF INTENTION

I reach out to those around me with love and an open heart. I have within me the power to create a life filled with precious connection to those around me. I release any blame and stand tall, knowing I have the power to change what doesn't work in my life. I focus on making my interactions with others a win-win situation for all of us.

Affirmation of the Day

I always choose the path with the heart.

> I commit 100% to each area of my life.
> I know that I count and I act as if I do.

MY LIFE IS RICH!

FAMILY

FRIENDS

HEALTH

PERSONAL GROWTH

SPIRITUAL GROWTH

ALONE TIME

RELATIONSHIP

CONTRIBUTION TO COMMUNITY

PLAYTIME

WORK

RISK OF THE DAY

TODAY I AM GRATEFUL FOR

Where do I belong today on my Pain-to-Power Chart?

▶ ▶

PAIN   **POWER**

I reach out to those around me with love and an open heart. I have within me the power to create a life filled with precious connection to those around me. I release any blame and stand tall, knowing I have the power to change what doesn't work in my life. I focus on making my interactions with others a win-win situation for all of us.

Affirmation of the Day

I give up my need to control everything around me.

I commit 100% to each area of my life.
I know that I count and I act as if I do.

MY LIFE IS RICH!

FAMILY

FRIENDS

HEALTH

PERSONAL GROWTH

SPIRITUAL GROWTH

ALONE TIME

RELATIONSHIP

CONTRIBUTION TO COMMUNITY

PLAYTIME

WORK

RISK OF THE DAY

TODAY I AM GRATEFUL FOR

Where do I belong today on my Pain-to-Power Chart?

▶ ▶

PAIN   **POWER**

STATEMENT OF INTENTION

I reach out to those around me with love and an open heart. I have within me the power to create a life filled with precious connection to those around me. I release any blame and stand tall, knowing I have the power to change what doesn't work in my life. I focus on making my interactions with others a win-win situation for all of us.

Affirmation of the Day

I reach out and invite others into my life.

I commit 100% to each area of my life.
I know that I count and I act as if I do.

MY LIFE IS RICH!

FAMILY

FRIENDS

HEALTH

PERSONAL GROWTH

SPIRITUAL GROWTH

ALONE TIME

RELATIONSHIP

CONTRIBUTION TO COMMUNITY

PLAYTIME

WORK

RISK OF THE DAY

TODAY I AM GRATEFUL FOR

Where do I belong today on my Pain-to-Power Chart?

▶ ▶

PAIN   **POWER**

STATEMENT OF INTENTION

I reach out to those around me with love and an open heart. I have within me the power to create a life filled with precious connection to those around me. I release any blame and stand tall, knowing I have the power to change what doesn't work in my life. I focus on making my interactions with others a win-win situation for all of us.

Affirmation of the Day

*Appreciation flows from my lips as I say thank you
to everyone around me.*

> I commit 100% to each area of my life.
> I know that I count and I act as if I do.

MY LIFE IS RICH!

FAMILY _____

FRIENDS _____

HEALTH _____

PERSONAL GROWTH _____

SPIRITUAL GROWTH _____

ALONE TIME _____

RELATIONSHIP _____

CONTRIBUTION TO COMMUNITY _____

PLAYTIME _____

WORK _____

_____

RISK OF THE DAY _____

TODAY I AM GRATEFUL FOR _____

_____

Where do I belong today on my Pain-to-Power Chart?

▶ ▶

PAIN   **POWER**

STATEMENT OF INTENTION

I reach out to those around me with love and an open heart. I have within me the power to create a life filled with precious connection to those around me. I release any blame and stand tall, knowing I have the power to change what doesn't work in my life. I focus on making my interactions with others a win-win situation for all of us.

Affirmation of the Day

I use every situation to spread more love in this world.

> I commit 100% to each area of my life.
> I know that I count and I act as if I do.

MY LIFE IS RICH!

FAMILY

FRIENDS

HEALTH

PERSONAL GROWTH

SPIRITUAL GROWTH

ALONE TIME

RELATIONSHIP

CONTRIBUTION TO COMMUNITY

PLAYTIME

WORK

RISK OF THE DAY

TODAY I AM GRATEFUL FOR

Where do I belong today on my Pain-to-Power Chart?

▶ ▶

PAIN   **POWER**

STATEMENT OF INTENTION

I reach out to those around me with love and an open heart. I have within me the power to create a life filled with precious connection to those around me. I release any blame and stand tall, knowing I have the power to change what doesn't work in my life. I focus on making my interactions with others a win-win situation for all of us.

Affirmation of the Day

I touch the world with love wherever I go.

I commit 100% to each area of my life.
I know that I count and I act as if I do.

MY LIFE IS RICH!

FAMILY

FRIENDS

HEALTH

PERSONAL GROWTH

SPIRITUAL GROWTH

ALONE TIME

RELATIONSHIP

CONTRIBUTION TO COMMUNITY

PLAYTIME

WORK

RISK OF THE DAY

TODAY I AM GRATEFUL FOR

Where do I belong today on my Pain-to-Power Chart?

▶ ▶

PAIN   POWER

STATEMENT OF INTENTION

I reach out to those around me with love and an open heart. I have within me the power to create a life filled with precious connection to those around me. I release any blame and stand tall, knowing I have the power to change what doesn't work in my life. I focus on making my interactions with others a win-win situation for all of us.

Affirmation of the Day

*Every loving action I take helps to heal the
hurts within and around me.*

> I commit 100% to each area of my life.
> I know that I count and I act as if I do.

MY LIFE IS RICH!

FAMILY

FRIENDS

HEALTH

PERSONAL GROWTH

SPIRITUAL GROWTH

ALONE TIME

RELATIONSHIP

CONTRIBUTION TO COMMUNITY

PLAYTIME

WORK

RISK OF THE DAY

TODAY I AM GRATEFUL FOR

Where do I belong today on my Pain-to-Power Chart?

▶ ▶

PAIN   **POWER**

sculpting my life I am sculpting my life I am sculpting my life I am sculpting m
sculpting my life I am sculpting my life I am sculpting my life I am sculpting m
sculpting my life I am sculpting my life I am sculpting my life I am sculpting m
scul   ulpting m
scul   ulpting m
scul   This week I focus on   ulpting m
scul   ulpting m
scul   ACTION   ulpting m
scul   ulpting m
scul   ulpting m
scul   ulpting m
scul   ulpting m

sculpting my life I am sculpting my life I am sculpting my life I am sculpting m
sculpting my life I am sculpting my life I am sculpting my life I am sculpting m
sculpting my life I am sculpting my life I am sculpting my life I am sculpting m
sculpting my life I am sculpting my life I am sculpting my life I am sculpting m
sculpting my life I am sculpting my life I am sculpting my life I am sculpting m
sculpting my life I am sculpting my life I am sculpting my life I am sculpting m
sculpting my life I am sculpting my life I am sculpting my life I am sculpting m
sculpting my life I am sculpting my life I am sculpting my life I am sculpting m
sculpting my life I am sculpting my life I am sculpting my life I am sculpting m
sculpting my life I am sculpting my life I am sculpting my life I am sculpting m
sculpting my life I am sculpting my life I am sculpting my life I am sculpting m
sculpting my life I am sculpting my life I am sculpting my life I am sculpting m
sculpting my life I am sculpting my life I am sculpting my life I am sculpting m
sculpting my life I am sculpting my life I am sculpting my life I am sculpting m
sculpting my life I am sculpting my life I am sculpting my life I am sculpting m
sculpting my life I am sculpting my life I am sculpting my life I am sculpting m
sculpting my life I am sculpting my life I am sculpting my life I am sculpting m
sculpting my life I am sculpting my life I am sculpting my life I am sculpting m
sculpting my life I am sculpting my life I am sculpting my life I am sculpting r
sculpting my life I am sculpting my life I am sculpting my life I am sculpting r

STATEMENT OF INTENTION

All that I ever need is in my power to create. I channel all my resources to find constructive, healthy ways to deal with all situations. With right action, I move easily and effortlessly towards all that is for my highest good. I act out of strength combined with love ... a winning combination for a joyful life.

Affirmation of the Day

I know that I count and I act as if I do.

> I commit 100% to each area of my life.
> I know that I count and I act as if I do.

MY LIFE IS RICH!

FAMILY

FRIENDS

HEALTH

PERSONAL GROWTH

SPIRITUAL GROWTH

ALONE TIME

RELATIONSHIP

CONTRIBUTION TO COMMUNITY

PLAYTIME

WORK

RISK OF THE DAY

TODAY I AM GRATEFUL FOR

Where do I belong today on my Pain-to-Power Chart?

PAIN ▶ **POWER**

STATEMENT OF INTENTION

All that I ever need is in my power to create. I channel all my resources to find constructive, healthy ways to deal with all situations. With right action, I move easily and effortlessly towards all that is for my highest good. I act out of strength combined with love … a winning combination for a joyful life.

Affirmation of the Day

*I am changing what doesn't work in my life ...
one step at a time.*

I commit 100% to each area of my life. I know that I count and I act as if I do.

MY LIFE IS RICH!

FAMILY _____

FRIENDS _____

HEALTH _____

PERSONAL GROWTH _____

SPIRITUAL GROWTH _____

ALONE TIME _____

RELATIONSHIP _____

CONTRIBUTION TO COMMUNITY _____

PLAYTIME _____

WORK _____

RISK OF THE DAY _____

TODAY I AM GRATEFUL FOR _____

Where do I belong today on my Pain-to-Power Chart?

▶ ▶
PAIN   **POWER**

STATEMENT OF INTENTION

All that I ever need is in my power to create. I channel all my resources to find constructive, healthy ways to deal with all situations. With right action, I move easily and effortlessly towards all that is for my highest good. I act out of strength combined with love ... a winning combination for a joyful life.

Affirmation of the Day

I feel the fear ... and do it anyway!

I commit 100% to each area of my life.
I know that I count and I act as if I do.

MY LIFE IS RICH!

FAMILY
....

FRIENDS
....

HEALTH
....

PERSONAL GROWTH
....

SPIRITUAL GROWTH
....

ALONE TIME
....

RELATIONSHIP
....

CONTRIBUTION TO COMMUNITY
....

PLAYTIME
....

WORK
....

RISK OF THE DAY
....

TODAY I AM GRATEFUL FOR
....

Where do I belong today on my Pain-to-Power Chart?

▶ ▶ ▶ ▶ ▶ ▶ ▶ ▶ ▶ ▶ ▶ ▶ ▶ ▶ ▶ ▶ ▶ ▶ ▶ ▶

PAIN   **POWER**

All that I ever need is in my power to create. I channel all my resources to find constructive, healthy ways to deal with all situations. With right action, I move easily and effortlessly towards all that is for my highest good. I act out of strength combined with love ... a winning combination for a joyful life.

Affirmation of the Day

*I let go of blame and take control of my reactions to
all experiences in my life.*

I commit 100% to each area of my life.
I know that I count and I act as if I do.

MY LIFE IS RICH!

FAMILY

FRIENDS

HEALTH

PERSONAL GROWTH

SPIRITUAL GROWTH

ALONE TIME

RELATIONSHIP

CONTRIBUTION TO COMMUNITY

PLAYTIME

WORK

RISK OF THE DAY

TODAY I AM GRATEFUL FOR

Where do I belong today on my Pain-to-Power Chart?

▶ ▶

PAIN   **POWER**

All that I ever need is in my power to create. I channel all my resources to find constructive, healthy ways to deal with all situations. With right action, I move easily and effortlessly towards all that is for my highest good. I act out of strength combined with love ... a winning combination for a joyful life.

Affirmation of the Day

*Step by step, I have the power to change all
that is not working in my life.*

I commit 100% to each area of my life.
I know that I count and I act as if I do.

MY LIFE IS RICH!

FAMILY

FRIENDS

HEALTH

PERSONAL GROWTH

SPIRITUAL GROWTH

ALONE TIME

RELATIONSHIP

CONTRIBUTION TO COMMUNITY

PLAYTIME

WORK

RISK OF THE DAY

TODAY I AM GRATEFUL FOR

Where do I belong today on my Pain-to-Power Chart?

▶ ▶

PAIN   **POWER**

All that I ever need is in my power to create. I channel all my resources to find constructive, healthy ways to deal with all situations. With right action, I move easily and effortlessly towards all that is for my highest good. I act out of strength combined with love ... a winning combination for a joyful life.

Affirmation of the Day

I am sculpting my life the way I want it to be.

I commit 100% to each area of my life.
I know that I count and I act as if I do.

MY LIFE IS RICH!

FAMILY

FRIENDS

HEALTH

PERSONAL GROWTH

SPIRITUAL GROWTH

ALONE TIME

RELATIONSHIP

CONTRIBUTION TO COMMUNITY

PLAYTIME

WORK

RISK OF THE DAY

TODAY I AM GRATEFUL FOR

Where do I belong today on my Pain-to-Power Chart?

▶ ▶

PAIN   **POWER**

STATEMENT OF INTENTION

All that I ever need is in my power to create. I channel all my resources to find constructive, healthy ways to deal with all situations. With right action, I move easily and effortlessly towards all that is for my highest good. I act out of strength combined with love ... a winning combination for a joyful life.

Affirmation of the Day

Step-by-step, I let go of what no longer works for me.

> I commit 100% to each area of my life.
> I know that I count and I act as if I do.

MY LIFE IS RICH!

FAMILY

FRIENDS

HEALTH

PERSONAL GROWTH

SPIRITUAL GROWTH

ALONE TIME

RELATIONSHIP

CONTRIBUTION TO COMMUNITY

PLAYTIME

WORK

RISK OF THE DAY

TODAY I AM GRATEFUL FOR

Where do I belong today on my Pain-to-Power Chart?

▶ ▶

PAIN   **POWER**

ate joy I radiate joy I radiate joy I radiate joy I radiate joy I radiate joy I radia
ate joy I radiate joy I radiate joy I radiate joy I radiate joy I radiate joy I radia
ate joy I radiate joy I radiate joy I radiate joy I radiate joy I radiate joy I radia

This week I focus on

RADIATING JOY

ate joy I radiate joy I radiate joy I radiate joy I radiate joy I radiate joy I radia
ate joy I radiate joy I radiate joy I radiate joy I radiate joy I radiate joy I radia
ate joy I radiate joy I radiate joy I radiate joy I radiate joy I radiate joy I radia
ate joy I radiate joy I radiate joy I radiate joy I radiate joy I radiate joy I radia
ate joy I radiate joy I radiate joy I radiate joy I radiate joy I radiate joy I radia
ate joy I radiate joy I radiate joy I radiate joy I radiate joy I radiate joy I radia
ate joy I radiate joy I radiate joy I radiate joy I radiate joy I radiate joy I radia
ate joy I radiate joy I radiate joy I radiate joy I radiate joy I radiate joy I radia
ate joy I radiate joy I radiate joy I radiate joy I radiate joy I radiate joy I radia
ate joy I radiate joy I radiate joy I radiate joy I radiate joy I radiate joy I radia
ate joy I radiate joy I radiate joy I radiate joy I radiate joy I radiate joy I radia
ate joy I radiate joy I radiate joy I radiate joy I radiate joy I radiate joy I radia
ate joy I radiate joy I radiate joy I radiate joy I radiate joy I radiate joy I radia
ate joy I radiate joy I radiate joy I radiate joy I radiate joy I radiate joy I radia
ate joy I radiate joy I radiate joy I radiate joy I radiate joy I radiate joy I radia
ate joy I radiate joy I radiate joy I radiate joy I radiate joy I radiate joy I radia
ate joy I radiate joy I radiate joy I radiate joy I radiate joy I radiate joy I radia
ate joy I radiate joy I radiate joy I radiate joy I radiate joy I radiate joy I radia
ate joy I radiate joy I radiate joy I radiate joy I radiate joy I radiate joy I radia
ate joy I radiate joy I radiate joy I radiate joy I radiate joy I radiate joy I radia

Each day I will remember to smile as I appreciate the goodness in my life. As I walk down the street, as I look around my home or office, as I talk on the phone, as I gaze out the window, as I eat my food, I will radiate joy. I have much to be joyful about today. With my smile, I spread that joy to everyone I meet.

Affirmation of the Day

*I am creating a better world for myself and
everyone around me.*

I commit 100% to each area of my life.
I know that I count and I act as if I do.

MY LIFE IS RICH!

FAMILY

FRIENDS

HEALTH

PERSONAL GROWTH

SPIRITUAL GROWTH

ALONE TIME

RELATIONSHIP

CONTRIBUTION TO COMMUNITY

PLAYTIME

WORK

RISK OF THE DAY

TODAY I AM GRATEFUL FOR

Where do I belong today on my Pain-to-Power Chart?

▶ ▶ ▶ ▶ ▶ ▶ ▶ ▶ ▶ ▶ ▶ ▶ ▶ ▶ ▶ ▶ ▶ ▶ ▶ ▶

PAIN   **POWER**

STATEMENT OF INTENTION

Each day I will remember to smile as I appreciate the goodness in my life. As I walk down the street, as I look around my home or office, as I talk on the phone, as I gaze out the window, as I eat my food, I will radiate joy. I have much to be joyful about today. With my smile, I spread that joy to everyone I meet.

Affirmation of the Day

I light the fire that warms the world.

> I commit 100% to each area of my life.
> I know that I count and I act as if I do.

MY LIFE IS RICH!

FAMILY

FRIENDS

HEALTH

PERSONAL GROWTH

SPIRITUAL GROWTH

ALONE TIME

RELATIONSHIP

CONTRIBUTION TO COMMUNITY

PLAYTIME

WORK

RISK OF THE DAY

TODAY I AM GRATEFUL FOR

Where do I belong today on my Pain-to-Power Chart?

▶ ▶

PAIN   **POWER**

STATEMENT OF INTENTION

Each day I will remember to smile as I appreciate the goodness in my life. As I walk down the street, as I look around my home or office, as I talk on the phone, as I gaze out the window, as I eat my food, I will radiate joy. I have much to be joyful about today. With my smile, I spread that joy to everyone I meet.

Affirmation of the Day

I act responsibly and lovingly towards myself and others.

> I commit 100% to each area of my life.
> I know that I count and I act as if I do.

MY LIFE IS RICH!

FAMILY

FRIENDS

HEALTH

PERSONAL GROWTH

SPIRITUAL GROWTH

ALONE TIME

RELATIONSHIP

CONTRIBUTION TO COMMUNITY

PLAYTIME

WORK

RISK OF THE DAY

TODAY I AM GRATEFUL FOR

Where do I belong today on my Pain-to-Power Chart?

▶▶▶▶▶▶▶▶▶▶▶▶▶▶▶▶▶▶▶▶▶▶

PAIN   **POWER**

STATEMENT OF INTENTION

Each day I will remember to smile as I appreciate the goodness in my life. As I walk down the street, as I look around my home or office, as I talk on the phone, as I gaze out the window, as I eat my food, I will radiate joy. I have much to be joyful about today. With my smile, I spread that joy to everyone I meet.

Affirmation of the Day

I warm the world with my love.

I commit 100% to each area of my life.
I know that I count and I act as if I do.

MY LIFE IS RICH!

FAMILY

FRIENDS

HEALTH

PERSONAL GROWTH

SPIRITUAL GROWTH

ALONE TIME

RELATIONSHIP

CONTRIBUTION TO COMMUNITY

PLAYTIME

WORK

RISK OF THE DAY

TODAY I AM GRATEFUL FOR

Where do I belong today on my Pain-to-Power Chart?

▶ ▶
PAIN   POWER

STATEMENT OF INTENTION

Each day I will remember to smile as I appreciate the goodness in my life. As I walk down the street, as I look around my home or office, as I talk on the phone, as I gaze out the window, as I eat my food, I will radiate joy. I have much to be joyful about today. With my smile, I spread that joy to everyone I meet.

Affirmation of the Day

I feel joy in the knowledge that my life has meaning.

> I commit 100% to each area of my life.
> I know that I count and I act as if I do.

MY LIFE IS RICH!

FAMILY

FRIENDS

HEALTH

PERSONAL GROWTH

SPIRITUAL GROWTH

ALONE TIME

RELATIONSHIP

CONTRIBUTION TO COMMUNITY

PLAYTIME

WORK

RISK OF THE DAY

TODAY I AM GRATEFUL FOR

Where do I belong today on my Pain-to-Power Chart?

▶ ▶

PAIN   **POWER**

Each day I will remember to smile as I appreciate the goodness in my life. As I walk down the street, as I look around my home or office, as I talk on the phone, as I gaze out the window, as I eat my food, I will radiate joy. I have much to be joyful about today. With my smile, I spread that joy to everyone I meet.

Affirmation of the Day

I radiate love and warmth everywhere I go.

I commit 100% to each area of my life.
I know that I count and I act as if I do.

MY LIFE IS RICH!

FAMILY

FRIENDS

HEALTH

PERSONAL GROWTH

SPIRITUAL GROWTH

ALONE TIME

RELATIONSHIP

CONTRIBUTION TO COMMUNITY

PLAYTIME

WORK

RISK OF THE DAY

TODAY I AM GRATEFUL FOR

Where do I belong today on my Pain-to-Power Chart?

▶ ▶

PAIN   **POWER**

Each day I will remember to smile as I appreciate the goodness in my life. As I walk down the street, as I look around my home or office, as I talk on the phone, as I gaze out the window, as I eat my food, I will radiate joy. I have much to be joyful about today. With my smile, I spread that joy to everyone I meet.

Affirmation of the Day

I love the world and the world loves me.

> I commit 100% to each area of my life.
> I know that I count and I act as if I do.

MY LIFE IS RICH!

FAMILY

FRIENDS

HEALTH

PERSONAL GROWTH

SPIRITUAL GROWTH

ALONE TIME

RELATIONSHIP

CONTRIBUTION TO COMMUNITY

PLAYTIME

WORK

RISK OF THE DAY

TODAY I AM GRATEFUL FOR

Where do I belong today on my Pain-to-Power Chart?

▶ ▶

PAIN   **POWER**

listen and I learn I listen and I learn and I listen and I learn I listen and I
n and I learn I listen and I learn I listen and I learn I listen and I learn I listen
I listen and I learn I listen and I learn I listen and I learn I listen and I learn

and   n I listen
I lis   I learn I
lear   This week I focus on   ten and I
n an   n I listen
I lis   INTUITION   en and I le
and   n I listen
I lis   I learn I
lear   ten and I

en and I learn I listen and I learn I listen and I learn I listen and I learn I listen
I listen and I learn I listen and I learn and I listen and I learn I listen and I le
n and I learn I listen and I learn I listen and I learn I listen and I learn I listen
I listen and I learn I listen and I learn I listen and I learn I listen and I learn
n and I learn I listen and I learn I listen and I learn I listen and I learn I listen
I listen and I learn I listen and I learn I listen and I learn I listen and I learn I
learn I listen and I learn and I listen and I learn I listen and I learn I listen and I
en and I learn I listen and I learn I listen and I learn I listen and I learn I listen
I listen and I learn I listen and I learn I listen and I learn I listen and I learn I
I learn I listen and I learn and I listen and I learn I listen and I learn I listen and I
en and I learn I listen and I learn I listen and I learn I listen and I learn I listen
n I listen and I learn I listen and I learn I listen and I learn and I listen and I I
n and I learn I listen and I learn I listen and I learn I listen and I learn I listen
n I listen and I learn I listen and I learn I listen and I learn I listen and I learn I
I learn and I listen and I learn I listen and I learn I listen and I learn I listen and I
en and I learn I listen and I learn I listen and I learn I listen and I learn I listen
n I listen and I learn I listen and I learn and I listen and I learn I listen and I I
n and I learn I listen and I learn I listen and I learn and I listen and I learn I listen
n I listen and I learn I listen and I learn I listen and I learn I listen and I learn
n I listen and I learn I listen and I learn I listen and I learn I listen and I learn
n and I learn I listen and I learn I listen and I learn I listen and I learn I listen
I listen and I learn I listen and I learn I listen and I learn I listen and I learn

STATEMENT OF INTENTION

I move beyond what my mind is capable of seeing. My Higher Self knows the infinite possibilities that live within and around me. I pay attention to the thoughts, feelings and situations that are there to lead me to my highest good. And I act accordingly. I trust I am being shown the way.

Affirmation of the Day

I look deeply and see the ultimate good in all things.

I commit 100% to each area of my life.
I know that I count and I act as if I do.

MY LIFE IS RICH!

FAMILY
_____

FRIENDS
_____

HEALTH
_____

PERSONAL GROWTH
_____

SPIRITUAL GROWTH
_____

ALONE TIME
_____

RELATIONSHIP
_____

CONTRIBUTION TO COMMUNITY
_____

PLAYTIME
_____

WORK

_____

RISK OF THE DAY
_____

TODAY I AM GRATEFUL FOR

_____

Where do I belong today on my Pain-to-Power Chart?

▷ ▷

PAIN   **POWER**

STATEMENT OF INTENTION

I move beyond what my mind is capable of seeing. My Higher Self knows the infinite possibilities that live within and around me. I pay attention to the thoughts, feelings and situations that are there to lead me to my highest good. And I act accordingly. I trust I am being shown the way.

Affirmation of the Day

*I am doing everything that needs to be done ...
one step at a time.*

I commit 100% to each area of my life.
I know that I count and I act as if I do.

MY LIFE IS RICH!

FAMILY

FRIENDS

HEALTH

PERSONAL GROWTH

SPIRITUAL GROWTH

ALONE TIME

RELATIONSHIP

CONTRIBUTION TO COMMUNITY

PLAYTIME

WORK

RISK OF THE DAY

TODAY I AM GRATEFUL FOR

Where do I belong today on my Pain-to-Power Chart?

▶▶▶▶▶▶▶▶▶▶▶▶▶▶▶▶▶▶▶▶▶

PAIN   **POWER**

STATEMENT OF INTENTION

I move beyond what my mind is capable of seeing. My Higher Self knows the infinite possibilities that live within and around me. I pay attention to the thoughts, feelings and situations that are there to lead me to my highest good. And I act accordingly. I trust I am being shown the way.

Affirmation of the Day

I touch the world and the world touches me.

> I commit 100% to each area of my life.
> I know that I count and I act as if I do.

MY LIFE IS RICH!

FAMILY

FRIENDS

HEALTH

PERSONAL GROWTH

SPIRITUAL GROWTH

ALONE TIME

RELATIONSHIP

CONTRIBUTION TO COMMUNITY

PLAYTIME

WORK

RISK OF THE DAY

TODAY I AM GRATEFUL FOR

Where do I belong today on my Pain-to-Power Chart?

▷▷▷▷▷▷▷▷▷▷▷▷▷▷▷▷▷▷▷▷▷▷▷
PAIN   POWER

STATEMENT OF INTENTION

I move beyond what my mind is capable of seeing. My Higher Self knows the infinite possibilities that live within and around me. I pay attention to the thoughts, feelings and situations that are there to lead me to my highest good. And I act accordingly. I trust I am being shown the way.

Affirmation of the Day

I move into the light and see the huge expanse of possibility.

> I commit 100% to each area of my life.
> I know that I count and I act as if I do.

MY LIFE IS RICH!

FAMILY

FRIENDS

HEALTH

PERSONAL GROWTH

SPIRITUAL GROWTH

ALONE TIME

RELATIONSHIP

CONTRIBUTION TO COMMUNITY

PLAYTIME

WORK

RISK OF THE DAY

TODAY I AM GRATEFUL FOR

Where do I belong today on my Pain-to-Power Chart?

▶ ▶

PAIN **POWER**

STATEMENT OF INTENTION

I move beyond what my mind is capable of seeing. My Higher Self knows the infinite possibilities that live within and around me. I pay attention to the thoughts, feelings and situations that are there to lead me to my highest good. And I act accordingly. I trust I am being shown the way.

Affirmation of the Day

Wherever I look, I notice the huge amount of love around me.

> I commit 100% to each area of my life.
> I know that I count and I act as if I do.

MY LIFE IS RICH!

FAMILY

FRIENDS

HEALTH

PERSONAL GROWTH

SPIRITUAL GROWTH

ALONE TIME

RELATIONSHIP

CONTRIBUTION TO COMMUNITY

PLAYTIME

WORK

RISK OF THE DAY

TODAY I AM GRATEFUL FOR

Where do I belong today on my Pain-to-Power Chart?

▶ ▶

PAIN   **POWER**

STATEMENT OF INTENTION

I move beyond what my mind is capable of seeing. My Higher Self knows the infinite possibilities that live within and around me. I pay attention to the thoughts, feelings and situations that are there to lead me to my highest good. And I act accordingly. I trust I am being shown the way.

Affirmation of the Day

I see beyond the petty into the bigger world of light and love.

I commit 100% to each area of my life.
I know that I count and I act as if I do.

MY LIFE IS RICH!

FAMILY

FRIENDS

HEALTH

PERSONAL GROWTH

SPIRITUAL GROWTH

ALONE TIME

RELATIONSHIP

CONTRIBUTION TO COMMUNITY

PLAYTIME

WORK

RISK OF THE DAY

TODAY I AM GRATEFUL FOR

Where do I belong today on my Pain-to-Power Chart?

▶ ▶

PAIN   **POWER**

STATEMENT OF INTENTION

I move beyond what my mind is capable of seeing. My Higher Self knows the infinite possibilities that live within and around me. I pay attention to the thoughts, feelings and situations that are there to lead me to my highest good. And I act accordingly. I trust I am being shown the way.

Affirmation of the Day

Each step takes me closer to the best of who I am.

I commit 100% to each area of my life.
I know that I count and I act as if I do.

MY LIFE IS RICH!

FAMILY

FRIENDS

HEALTH

PERSONAL GROWTH

SPIRITUAL GROWTH

ALONE TIME

RELATIONSHIP

CONTRIBUTION TO COMMUNITY

PLAYTIME

WORK

RISK OF THE DAY

TODAY I AM GRATEFUL FOR

Where do I belong today on my Pain-to-Power Chart?

▶ ▶

PAIN   **POWER**

the light is within me the light is within me the light is within me the light is with
the light is within me the light is within me the light is within me the light is with
ght is within me the light is within me the light is within me the light is with

light i
ight
ight
ight
ight
ight
ight
ight
ight

This week I focus on

MY HIGHER

SELF

nt is with
nt is with
nt is with
nt is with
nt is with
nt is with
nt is with
nt is with
nt is with

light is within me the light is within me the light is within me the light is with
light is within me the light is within me the light is within me the light is with
light is within me the light is within me the light is within me the light is with
light is within me the light is within me the light is within me the light is with
light is within me the light is within me the light is within me the light is with
light is within me the light is within me the light is within me the light is with
light is within me the light is within me the light is within me the light is with
light is within me the light is within me the light is within me the light is with
light is within me the light is within me the light is within me the light is with
light is within me the light is within me the light is within me the light is with
light is within me the light is within me the light is within me the light is with
light is within me the light is within me the light is within me the light is with
light is within me the light is within me the light is within me the light is with
light is within me the light is within me the light is within me the light is with
light is within me the light is within me the light is within me the light is with
light is within me the light is within me the light is within me the light is with
light is within me the light is within me the light is within me the light is with
light is within me the light is within me the light is within me the light is with
light is within me the light is within me The light is within me the light is with
light is within me the light is within me The light is within me the light is with

I tune into the very best of who I am ... my Higher Self. I am comforted by the fact that there lives within me this joyful place of loving, giving, appreciation, power and all good things. Little-by-little, I am discovering the powerful tools that take me to this wonderful place of healing and light.

Affirmation of the Day

I am grateful for the opportunity that all experiences offer me.

> I commit 100% to each area of my life.
> I know that I count and I act as if I do.

MY LIFE IS RICH!

FAMILY

FRIENDS

HEALTH

PERSONAL GROWTH

SPIRITUAL GROWTH

ALONE TIME

RELATIONSHIP

CONTRIBUTION TO COMMUNITY

PLAYTIME

WORK

RISK OF THE DAY

TODAY I AM GRATEFUL FOR

Where do I belong today on my Pain-to-Power Chart?

▶ ▶

PAIN   **POWER**

I tune into the very best of who I am ... my Higher Self. I am comforted by the fact that there lives within me this joyful place of loving, giving, appreciation, power and all good things. Little-by-little, I am discovering the powerful tools that take me to this wonderful place of healing and light.

Affirmation of the Day

*I rise above the petty to a more powerful and
loving way of being.*

I commit 100% to each area of my life.
I know that I count and I act as if I do.

MY LIFE IS RICH!

FAMILY

FRIENDS

HEALTH

PERSONAL GROWTH

SPIRITUAL GROWTH

ALONE TIME

RELATIONSHIP

CONTRIBUTION TO COMMUNITY

PLAYTIME

WORK

RISK OF THE DAY

TODAY I AM GRATEFUL FOR

Where do I belong today on my Pain-to-Power Chart?

▶ ▶

PAIN   **POWER**

STATEMENT OF INTENTION

I tune into the very best of who I am ... my Higher Self. I am comforted by the fact that there lives within me this joyful place of loving, giving, appreciation, power and all good things. Little-by-little, I am discovering the powerful tools that take me to this wonderful place of healing and light.

Affirmation of the Day

I peacefully allow my life to unfold.

> I commit 100% to each area of my life.
> I know that I count and I act as if I do.

MY LIFE IS RICH!

FAMILY

FRIENDS

HEALTH

PERSONAL GROWTH

SPIRITUAL GROWTH

ALONE TIME

RELATIONSHIP

CONTRIBUTION TO COMMUNITY

PLAYTIME

WORK

RISK OF THE DAY

TODAY I AM GRATEFUL FOR

Where do I belong today on my Pain-to-Power Chart?

▶ ▶

PAIN   **POWER**

STATEMENT OF INTENTION

I tune into the very best of who I am ... my Higher Self. I am comforted by the fact that there lives within me this joyful place of loving, giving, appreciation, power and all good things. Little-by-little, I am discovering the powerful tools that take me to this wonderful place of healing and light.

Affirmation of the Day

*Within me is an endless source of wisdom that will help me
handle all that needs to be handled.*

> I commit 100% to each area of my life.
> I know that I count and I act as if I do.

MY LIFE IS RICH!

FAMILY

FRIENDS

HEALTH

PERSONAL GROWTH

SPIRITUAL GROWTH

ALONE TIME

RELATIONSHIP

CONTRIBUTION TO COMMUNITY

PLAYTIME

WORK

RISK OF THE DAY

TODAY I AM GRATEFUL FOR

Where do I belong today on my Pain-to-Power Chart?

▶ ▶

PAIN   **POWER**

STATEMENT OF INTENTION

I tune into the very best of who I am ... my Higher Self. I am comforted by the fact that there lives within me this joyful place of loving, giving, appreciation, power and all good things. Little-by-little, I am discovering the powerful tools that take me to this wonderful place of healing and light.

Affirmation of the Day

*I look at the opportunity for growth that
all experiences offer me.*

I commit 100% to each area of my life.
I know that I count and I act as if I do.

MY LIFE IS RICH!

FAMILY
....

FRIENDS
....

HEALTH
....

PERSONAL GROWTH
....

SPIRITUAL GROWTH
....

ALONE TIME
....

RELATIONSHIP
....

CONTRIBUTION TO COMMUNITY
....

PLAYTIME
....

WORK

....

RISK OF THE DAY
....

TODAY I AM GRATEFUL FOR

....

Where do I belong today on my Pain-to-Power Chart?

▶ ▶
PAIN   **POWER**

STATEMENT OF INTENTION

I tune into the very best of who I am ... my Higher Self. I am comforted by the fact that there lives within me this joyful place of loving, giving, appreciation, power and all good things. Little-by-little, I am discovering the powerful tools that take me to this wonderful place of healing and light.

Affirmation of the Day

I listen for inner guidance and I move towards the path of love.

> I commit 100% to each area of my life.
> I know that I count and I act as if I do.

MY LIFE IS RICH!

FAMILY
_____

FRIENDS
_____

HEALTH
_____

PERSONAL GROWTH
_____

SPIRITUAL GROWTH
_____

ALONE TIME
_____

RELATIONSHIP
_____

CONTRIBUTION TO COMMUNITY
_____

PLAYTIME
_____

WORK
_____

_____

RISK OF THE DAY
_____

TODAY I AM GRATEFUL FOR
_____

Where do I belong today on my Pain-to-Power Chart?

▶ ▶

PAIN   **POWER**

STATEMENT OF INTENTION

I tune into the very best of who I am ... my Higher Self. I am comforted by the fact that there lives within me this joyful place of loving, giving, appreciation, power and all good things. Little-by-little, I am discovering the powerful tools that take me to this wonderful place of healing and light.

Affirmation of the Day

My highest priority is to follow the path with the heart.

> I commit 100% to each area of my life.
> I know that I count and I act as if I do.

MY LIFE IS RICH!

FAMILY

FRIENDS

HEALTH

PERSONAL GROWTH

SPIRITUAL GROWTH

ALONE TIME

RELATIONSHIP

CONTRIBUTION TO COMMUNITY

PLAYTIME

WORK

RISK OF THE DAY

TODAY I AM GRATEFUL FOR

Where do I belong today on my Pain-to-Power Chart?

▶▶▶▶▶▶▶▶▶▶▶▶▶▶▶▶▶▶▶▶▶

PAIN   **POWER**

and trust I let go and trust I let go and trust I let go and trust I let go and t
and trust I let go and trust I let go and trust I let go and trust I let go and t
and trust I let go and trust I let go and trust I let go and trust I let go and t

This week I focus on
TRUST

o and trust I let go and trust I let go and trust I let go and trust I let go and t
o and trust I let go and trust I let go and trust I let go and trust I let go and t
o and trust I let go and trust I let go and trust I let go and trust I let go and t
o and trust I let go and trust I let go and trust I let go and trust I let go and t
o and trust I let go and trust I let go and trust I let go and trust I let go and t
o and trust I let go and trust I let go and trust I let go and trust I let go and t
o and trust I let go and trust I let go and trust I let go and trust I let go and t
o and trust I let go and trust I let go and trust I let go and trust I let go and t
o and trust I let go and trust I let go and trust I let go and trust I let go and t
o and trust I let go and trust I let go and trust I let go and trust I let go and t
o and trust I let go and trust I let go and trust I let go and trust I let go and t
o and trust I let go and trust I let go and trust I let go and trust I let go and t
o and trust I let go and trust I let go and trust I let go and trust I let go and t
o and trust I let go and trust I let go and trust I let go and trust I let go and t
o and trust I let go and trust I let go and trust I let go and trust I let go and
o and trust I let go and trust I let go and trust I let go and trust I let go and
o and trust I let go and trust I let go and trust I let go and trust I let go and
o and trust I let go and trust I let go and trust I let go and trust I let go and
o and trust I let go and trust I let go and trust I let go and trust I let go and

STATEMENT OF INTENTION

I let go of my need to control everything in my life. I do my very best and then let go of the outcome. I trust that from all things that happen ... good and bad ... I will learn and I will grow. I say 'YES!' to it all. I always remember that I am powerful and I am loving and I have nothing to fear.

Affirmation of the Day

I trust that it's all happening for my highest good.

> I commit 100% to each area of my life.
> I know that I count and I act as if I do.

MY LIFE IS RICH!

FAMILY

FRIENDS

HEALTH

PERSONAL GROWTH

SPIRITUAL GROWTH

ALONE TIME

RELATIONSHIP

CONTRIBUTION TO COMMUNITY

PLAYTIME

WORK

RISK OF THE DAY

TODAY I AM GRATEFUL FOR

Where do I belong today on my Pain-to-Power Chart?

▶ ▶

PAIN   **POWER**

STATEMENT OF INTENTION

I let go of my need to control everything in my life. I do my very best and then let go of the outcome. I trust that from all things that happen ... good and bad ... I will learn and I will grow. I say 'YES!' to it all. I always remember that I am powerful and I am loving and I have nothing to fear.

Affirmation of the Day

I let go and allow the river to carry me to new adventures.

> I commit 100% to each area of my life.
> I know that I count and I act as if I do.

MY LIFE IS RICH!

FAMILY

FRIENDS

HEALTH

PERSONAL GROWTH

SPIRITUAL GROWTH

ALONE TIME

RELATIONSHIP

CONTRIBUTION TO COMMUNITY

PLAYTIME

WORK

RISK OF THE DAY

TODAY I AM GRATEFUL FOR

Where do I belong today on my Pain-to-Power Chart?

▶ ▶

PAIN   **POWER**

STATEMENT OF INTENTION

I let go of my need to control everything in my life. I do my very best and then let go of the outcome. I trust that from all things that happen ... good and bad ... I will learn and I will grow. I say 'YES!' to it all. I always remember that I am powerful and I am loving and I have nothing to fear.

Affirmation of the Day

I trust I will say exactly what needs to be said.

> I commit 100% to each area of my life.
> I know that I count and I act as if I do.

MY LIFE IS RICH!

FAMILY

FRIENDS

HEALTH

PERSONAL GROWTH

SPIRITUAL GROWTH

ALONE TIME

RELATIONSHIP

CONTRIBUTION TO COMMUNITY

PLAYTIME

WORK

RISK OF THE DAY

TODAY I AM GRATEFUL FOR

Where do I belong today on my Pain-to-Power Chart?

▶ ▶

PAIN   **POWER**

STATEMENT OF INTENTION

I let go of my need to control everything in my life. I do my very best and then let go of the outcome. I trust that from all things that happen ... good and bad ... I will learn and I will grow. I say 'YES!' to it all. I always remember that I am powerful and I am loving and I have nothing to fear.

Affirmation of the Day

I let go and I trust that it's all happening perfectly.

> I commit 100% to each area of my life.
> I know that I count and I act as if I do.

MY LIFE IS RICH!

FAMILY

FRIENDS

HEALTH

PERSONAL GROWTH

SPIRITUAL GROWTH

ALONE TIME

RELATIONSHIP

CONTRIBUTION TO COMMUNITY

PLAYTIME

WORK

RISK OF THE DAY

TODAY I AM GRATEFUL FOR

Where do I belong today on my Pain-to-Power Chart?

▶ ▶

PAIN   **POWER**

I let go of my need to control everything in my life. I do my very best and then let go of the outcome. I trust that from all things that happen ... good and bad ... I will learn and I will grow. I say 'YES!' to it all. I always remember that I am powerful and I am loving and I have nothing to fear.

Affirmation of the Day

I do my best and let go of the outcome.

I commit 100% to each area of my life.
I know that I count and I act as if I do.

MY LIFE IS RICH!

FAMILY

FRIENDS

HEALTH

PERSONAL GROWTH

SPIRITUAL GROWTH

ALONE TIME

RELATIONSHIP

CONTRIBUTION TO COMMUNITY

PLAYTIME

WORK

RISK OF THE DAY

TODAY I AM GRATEFUL FOR

Where do I belong today on my Pain-to-Power Chart?

▶ ▶

PAIN   **POWER**

STATEMENT OF INTENTION

I let go of my need to control everything in my life. I do my very best and then let go of the outcome. I trust that from all things that happen ... good and bad ... I will learn and I will grow. I say 'YES!' to it all. I always remember that I am powerful and I am loving and I have nothing to fear.

Affirmation of the Day

I let go of my resistance and allow in new possibilities.

> I commit 100% to each area of my life.
> I know that I count and I act as if I do.

MY LIFE IS RICH!

FAMILY

FRIENDS

HEALTH

PERSONAL GROWTH

SPIRITUAL GROWTH

ALONE TIME

RELATIONSHIP

CONTRIBUTION TO COMMUNITY

PLAYTIME

WORK

RISK OF THE DAY

TODAY I AM GRATEFUL FOR

Where do I belong today on my Pain-to-Power Chart?

▶ ▶

PAIN   **POWER**

I let go of my need to control everything in my life. I do my very best and then let go of the outcome. I trust that from all things that happen ... good and bad ... I will learn and I will grow. I say 'YES!' to it all. I always remember that I am powerful and I am loving and I have nothing to fear.

Affirmation of the Day

I learn and grow from all life experiences.

> I commit 100% to each area of my life.
> I know that I count and I act as if I do.

MY LIFE IS RICH!

FAMILY

FRIENDS

HEALTH

PERSONAL GROWTH

SPIRITUAL GROWTH

ALONE TIME

RELATIONSHIP

CONTRIBUTION TO COMMUNITY

PLAYTIME

WORK

RISK OF THE DAY

TODAY I AM GRATEFUL FOR

Where do I belong today on my Pain-to-Power Chart?

▶ ▶ ▶ ▶ ▶ ▶ ▶ ▶ ▶ ▶ ▶ ▶ ▶ ▶ ▶ ▶ ▶ ▶ ▶ ▶

PAIN   **POWER**

you I love you I love you I love you I love you I love you I love you I love you
love you I love you I love you I love you I love you I love you I love you I love
you I love you I love you I love you I love you I love you I love you I love you
love you I love you I love you I love you I love you I love you

This week I focus on

LOVE

love you I love you I love you I love you I love you I love you I love you I love
you I love you I love you I love you I love you I love you I love you I love you
love you I love you I love you I love you I love you I love you I love you I love
you I love you I love you I love you I love you I love you I love you I love you
love you I love you I love you I love you I love you I love you I love you I love
you I love you I love you I love you I love you I love you I love you I love you
love you I love you I love you I love you I love you I love you I love you I love
you I love you I love you I love you I love you I love you I love you I love you
love you I love you I love you I love you I love you I love you I love you I love
you I love you I love you I love you I love you I love you I love you I love you
love you I love you I love you I love you I love you I love you I love you I love
you I love you I love you I love you I love you I love you I love you I love you
love you I love you I love you I love you I love you I love you I love you I love
you I love you I love you I love you I love you I love you I love you I love you
love you I love you I love you I love you I love you I love you I love you I love
you I love you I love you I love you I love you I love you I love you I love you
love you I love you I love you I love you I love you I love you I love you I love
you I love you I love you I love you I love you I love you I love you I love you
love you I love you I love you I love you I love you I love you I love you I love

I am getting in touch with the huge amount of love I hold within my being. As I interact with people in my life, I silently project the thought, 'I love you'. I send this healing thought even to those who have caused me pain. In sending love to the world, I am filling my own heart with love as well. How sweet it is!

Affirmation of the Day

I am a lover-in-training and I am learning my lessons well.

> I commit 100% to each area of my life.
> I know that I count and I act as if I do.

MY LIFE IS RICH!

FAMILY

FRIENDS

HEALTH

PERSONAL GROWTH

SPIRITUAL GROWTH

ALONE TIME

RELATIONSHIP

CONTRIBUTION TO COMMUNITY

PLAYTIME

WORK

RISK OF THE DAY

TODAY I AM GRATEFUL FOR

Where do I belong today on my Pain-to-Power Chart?

▶ ▶

PAIN   **POWER**

I am getting in touch with the huge amount of love I hold within my being. As I interact with people in my life, I silently project the thought, 'I love you'. I send this healing thought even to those who have caused me pain. In sending love to the world, I am filling my own heart with love as well. How sweet it is!

Affirmation of the Day

I give from a place of love rather than expectation.

> I commit 100% to each area of my life.
> I know that I count and I act as if I do.

MY LIFE IS RICH!

FAMILY

FRIENDS

HEALTH

PERSONAL GROWTH

SPIRITUAL GROWTH

ALONE TIME

RELATIONSHIP

CONTRIBUTION TO COMMUNITY

PLAYTIME

WORK

RISK OF THE DAY

TODAY I AM GRATEFUL FOR

Where do I belong today on my Pain-to-Power Chart?

▶ ▶

PAIN   **POWER**

STATEMENT OF INTENTION

I am getting in touch with the huge amount of love I hold within my being. As I interact with people in my life, I silently project the thought, 'I love you.' I send this healing thought even to those who have caused me pain. In sending love to the world, I am filling my own heart with love as well. How sweet it is!

Affirmation of the Day

*All situations offer me the opportunity to
become a more loving person.*

I commit 100% to each area of my life.
I know that I count and I act as if I do.

MY LIFE IS RICH!

FAMILY

FRIENDS

HEALTH

PERSONAL GROWTH

SPIRITUAL GROWTH

ALONE TIME

RELATIONSHIP

CONTRIBUTION TO COMMUNITY

PLAYTIME

WORK

RISK OF THE DAY

TODAY I AM GRATEFUL FOR

Where do I belong today on my Pain-to-Power Chart?

▶ ▶

PAIN　　　　　　　　　　　　　　　　　**POWER**

STATEMENT OF INTENTION

I am getting in touch with the huge amount of love I hold within my being. As I interact with people in my life, I silently project the thought, 'I love you'. I send this healing thought even to those who have caused me pain. In sending love to the world, I am filling my own heart with love as well. How sweet it is!

Affirmation of the Day

I was born to use my loving power.

> I commit 100% to each area of my life.
> I know that I count and I act as if I do.

MY LIFE IS RICH!

FAMILY

FRIENDS

HEALTH

PERSONAL GROWTH

SPIRITUAL GROWTH

ALONE TIME

RELATIONSHIP

CONTRIBUTION TO COMMUNITY

PLAYTIME

WORK

RISK OF THE DAY

TODAY I AM GRATEFUL FOR

Where do I belong today on my Pain-to-Power Chart?

▶ ▶

PAIN   **POWER**

I am getting in touch with the huge amount of love I hold within my being. As I interact with people in my life, I silently project the thought, 'I love you'. I send this healing thought even to those who have caused me pain. In sending love to the world, I am filling my own heart with love as well. How sweet it is!

Affirmation of the Day

I commit to putting more love into everything I do.

> I commit 100% to each area of my life.
> I know that I count and I act as if I do.

MY LIFE IS RICH!

FAMILY

FRIENDS

HEALTH

PERSONAL GROWTH

SPIRITUAL GROWTH

ALONE TIME

RELATIONSHIP

CONTRIBUTION TO COMMUNITY

PLAYTIME

WORK

RISK OF THE DAY

TODAY I AM GRATEFUL FOR

Where do I belong today on my Pain-to-Power Chart?

▶ ▶

PAIN   **POWER**

STATEMENT OF INTENTION

I am getting in touch with the huge amount of love I hold within my being. As I interact with people in my life, I silently project the thought, 'I love you'. I send this healing thought even to those who have caused me pain. In sending love to the world, I am filling my own heart with love as well. How sweet it is!

Affirmation of the Day

The love in my life, begins with me.

> I commit 100% to each area of my life.
> I know that I count and I act as if I do.

MY LIFE IS RICH!

FAMILY

FRIENDS

HEALTH

PERSONAL GROWTH

SPIRITUAL GROWTH

ALONE TIME

RELATIONSHIP

CONTRIBUTION TO COMMUNITY

PLAYTIME

WORK

RISK OF THE DAY

TODAY I AM GRATEFUL FOR

Where do I belong today on my Pain-to-Power Chart?

▶ ▶

PAIN   **POWER**

STATEMENT OF INTENTION

I am getting in touch with the huge amount of love I hold within my being. As I interact with people in my life, I silently project the thought, 'I love you'. I send this healing thought even to those who have caused me pain. In sending love to the world, I am filling my own heart with love as well. How sweet it is!

Affirmation of the Day

My being a loving person depends only on me.

> I commit 100% to each area of my life.
> I know that I count and I act as if I do.

MY LIFE IS RICH!

FAMILY

FRIENDS

HEALTH

PERSONAL GROWTH

SPIRITUAL GROWTH

ALONE TIME

RELATIONSHIP

CONTRIBUTION TO COMMUNITY

PLAYTIME

WORK

RISK OF THE DAY

TODAY I AM GRATEFUL FOR

Where do I belong today on my Pain-to-Power Chart?

▶ ▶ ▶ ▶ ▶ ▶ ▶ ▶ ▶ ▶ ▶ ▶ ▶ ▶ ▶ ▶ ▶ ▶ ▶ ▶

PAIN   **POWER**

ening perfectly it's all happening perfectly it's all happening perfectly i
ening perfectly it's all happening perfectly it's all happening perfectly i
ening perfectly it's all happening perfectly it's all happening perfectly i
enin   erfectly i
enin   erfectly i
enin   This week I focus on   erfectly i
enin   erfectly i
enin   INNER PEACE   erfectly i
enin   erfectly i
enin   erfectly i
enin   erfectly i

ening perfectly it's all happening perfectly it's all happening perfectly i
ening perfectly it's all happening perfectly it's all happening perfectly i
ening perfectly it's all happening perfectly it's all happening perfectly i
ening perfectly it's all happening perfectly it's all happening perfectly i
ening perfectly it's all happening perfectly it's all happening perfectly i
ening perfectly it's all happening perfectly it's all happening perfectly i
ening perfectly it's all happening perfectly it's all happening perfectly i
ening perfectly it's all happening perfectly it's all happening perfectly i
ening perfectly it's all happening perfectly it's all happening perfectly i
ening perfectly it's all happening perfectly it's all happening perfectly i
ening perfectly it's all happening perfectly it's all happening perfectly i
ening perfectly it's all happening perfectly it's all happening perfectly i
ening perfectly it's all happening perfectly it's all happening perfectly i
ening perfectly it's all happening perfectly it's all happening perfectly i
ening perfectly it's all happening perfectly it's all happening perfectly i
ening perfectly it's all happening perfectly it's all happening perfectly i
ening perfectly it's all happening perfectly it's all happening perfectly i
ening perfectly it's all happening perfectly it's all happening perfectly i
ening perfectly it's all happening perfectly it's all happening perfectly i
ening perfectly it's all happening perfectly it's all happening perfectly i
ening perfectly it's all happening perfectly it's all happening perfectly i
ening perfectly it's all happening perfectly it's all happening perfectly i
ening perfectly it's all happening perfectly it's all happening perfectly i

Now is the time to allow peace into my heart. Whatever happens in my life, I'll handle it. I'll make it a triumph. While I can't see the 'Grand Design', I rest knowing it's all happening perfectly. In all things, I am supported and protected by the powerful energy of my Higher Self. I let go of the worry. I am at peace.

Affirmation of the Day

I release the past and focus on the beauty of the now.

> I commit 100% to each area of my life.
> I know that I count and I act as if I do.

MY LIFE IS RICH!

FAMILY

FRIENDS

HEALTH

PERSONAL GROWTH

SPIRITUAL GROWTH

ALONE TIME

RELATIONSHIP

CONTRIBUTION TO COMMUNITY

PLAYTIME

WORK

RISK OF THE DAY

TODAY I AM GRATEFUL FOR

Where do I belong today on my Pain-to-Power Chart?

▶ ▶

PAIN   **POWER**

STATEMENT OF INTENTION

Now is the time to allow peace into my heart. Whatever happens in my life, I'll handle it. I'll make it a triumph. While I can't see the 'Grand Design', I rest knowing it's all happening perfectly. In all things, I am supported and protected by the powerful energy of my Higher Self. I let go of the worry. I am at peace.

Affirmation of the Day

*I put aside all stressful thoughts and focus on
what is beautiful now.*

> I commit 100% to each area of my life.
> I know that I count and I act as if I do.

MY LIFE IS RICH!

FAMILY

FRIENDS

HEALTH

PERSONAL GROWTH

SPIRITUAL GROWTH

ALONE TIME

RELATIONSHIP

CONTRIBUTION TO COMMUNITY

PLAYTIME

WORK

RISK OF THE DAY

TODAY I AM GRATEFUL FOR

Where do I belong today on my Pain-to-Power Chart?

▶ ▶

PAIN   **POWER**

Now is the time to allow peace into my heart. Whatever happens in my life, I'll handle it. I'll make it a triumph. While I can't see the 'Grand Design', I rest knowing it's all happening perfectly. In all things, I am supported and protected by the powerful energy of my Higher Self. I let go of the worry. I am at peace.

Affirmation of the Day

*I take a deep breath and cut the cord to
any unhealthy dependency.*

> I commit 100% to each area of my life.
> I know that I count and I act as if I do.

MY LIFE IS RICH!

FAMILY

FRIENDS

HEALTH

PERSONAL GROWTH

SPIRITUAL GROWTH

ALONE TIME

RELATIONSHIP

CONTRIBUTION TO COMMUNITY

PLAYTIME

WORK

RISK OF THE DAY

TODAY I AM GRATEFUL FOR

Where do I belong today on my Pain-to-Power Chart?

▶ ▶

PAIN   **POWER**

STATEMENT OF INTENTION

Now is the time to allow peace into my heart. Whatever happens in my life, I'll handle it. I'll make it a triumph. While I can't see the 'Grand Design', I rest knowing it's all happening perfectly. In all things, I am supported and protected by the powerful energy of my Higher Self. I let go of the worry. I am at peace.

Affirmation of the Day

I always have the inner strength to find my way.

> I commit 100% to each area of my life.
> I know that I count and I act as if I do.

MY LIFE IS RICH!

FAMILY ....

FRIENDS ....

HEALTH ....

PERSONAL GROWTH ....

SPIRITUAL GROWTH ....

ALONE TIME ....

RELATIONSHIP ....

CONTRIBUTION TO COMMUNITY ....

PLAYTIME ....

WORK ....

....

RISK OF THE DAY ....

TODAY I AM GRATEFUL FOR ....

....

Where do I belong today on my Pain-to-Power Chart?

▶ ▶

PAIN   **POWER**

STATEMENT OF INTENTION

Now is the time to allow peace into my heart. Whatever happens in my life, I'll handle it. I'll make it a triumph. While I can't see the 'Grand Design', I rest knowing it's all happening perfectly. In all things, I am supported and protected by the powerful energy of my Higher Self. I let go of the worry. I am at peace.

Affirmation of the Day

One step at a time is enough for me.

> I commit 100% to each area of my life.
> I know that I count and I act as if I do.

MY LIFE IS RICH!

FAMILY

FRIENDS

HEALTH

PERSONAL GROWTH

SPIRITUAL GROWTH

ALONE TIME

RELATIONSHIP

CONTRIBUTION TO COMMUNITY

PLAYTIME

WORK

RISK OF THE DAY

TODAY I AM GRATEFUL FOR

Where do I belong today on my Pain-to-Power Chart?

▶ ▶ ▶ ▶ ▶ ▶ ▶ ▶ ▶ ▶ ▶ ▶ ▶ ▶ ▶ ▶ ▶ ▶ ▶ ▶

PAIN   **POWER**

STATEMENT OF INTENTION

Now is the time to allow peace into my heart. Whatever happens in my life, I'll handle it. I'll make it a triumph. While I can't see the 'Grand Design', I rest knowing it's all happening perfectly. In all things, I am supported and protected by the powerful energy of my Higher Self. I let go of the worry. I am at peace.

Affirmation of the Day

Although all may be stressful around me,
I remain peaceful within me.

> I commit 100% to each area of my life.
> I know that I count and I act as if I do.

MY LIFE IS RICH!

FAMILY

FRIENDS

HEALTH

PERSONAL GROWTH

SPIRITUAL GROWTH

ALONE TIME

RELATIONSHIP

CONTRIBUTION TO COMMUNITY

PLAYTIME

WORK

RISK OF THE DAY

TODAY I AM GRATEFUL FOR

Where do I belong today on my Pain-to-Power Chart?

▶ ▶

PAIN   **POWER**

STATEMENT OF INTENTION

Now is the time to allow peace into my heart. Whatever happens in my life, I'll handle it. I'll make it a triumph. While I can't see the 'Grand Design', I rest knowing it's all happening perfectly. In all things, I am supported and protected by the powerful energy of my Higher Self. I let go of the worry. I am at peace.

Affirmation of the Day

*I am creating a feeling of peace within my body
and within my mind.*

> I commit 100% to each area of my life.
> I know that I count and I act as if I do.

MY LIFE IS RICH!

FAMILY

FRIENDS

HEALTH

PERSONAL GROWTH

SPIRITUAL GROWTH

ALONE TIME

RELATIONSHIP

CONTRIBUTION TO COMMUNITY

PLAYTIME

WORK

RISK OF THE DAY

TODAY I AM GRATEFUL FOR

Where do I belong today on my Pain-to-Power Chart?

▶ ▶

PAIN   **POWER**

Huge! Life is Huge! Life is Huge! Life is Huge! Life is Huge! Life is Huge! L
! Life is Huge! Life is Huge! Life is Huge! Life is Huge! Life is Huge! Life is H
s Huge! Life is Huge! Life is Huge! Life is Huge! Life is Huge! Life is Huge! L
! Lif   ! Life is H
s Hu   s Huge! L

This week I focus on

THE GIFT
OF LIFE

s Hu   s Huge! L
! Lif   ! Life is H
s Hu   s Huge! L
! Life is Huge! Life is Huge! Life is Huge! Life is Huge! Life is Huge! Life is H
s Huge! Life is Huge! Life is Huge! Life is Huge! Life is Huge! Life is Huge! L
! Life is Huge! Life is Huge! Life is Huge! Life is Huge! Life is Huge! Life is H
s Huge! Life is Huge! Life is Huge! Life is Huge! Life is Huge! Life is Huge! L
! Life is Huge! Life is Huge! Life is Huge! Life is Huge! Life is Huge! Life is H
is Huge! Life is Huge! Life is Huge! Life is Huge! Life is Huge! Life is Huge! L
! Life is Huge! Life is Huge! Life is Huge! Life is Huge! Life is Huge! Life is H
is Huge! Life is Huge! Life is Huge! Life is Huge! Life is Huge! Life is Huge! L
! Life is Huge! Life is Huge! Life is Huge! Life is Huge! Life is Huge! Life is H
is Huge! Life is Huge! Life is Huge! Life is Huge! Life is Huge! Life is Huge! L
! Life is Huge! Life is Huge! Life is Huge! Life is Huge! Life is Huge! Life is H
is Huge! Life is Huge! Life is Huge! Life is Huge! Life is Huge! Life is Huge! L
! Life is Huge! Life is Huge! Life is Huge! Life is Huge! Life is Huge! Life is H
is Huge! Life is Huge! Life is Huge! Life is Huge! Life is Huge! Life is Huge! L
! Life is Huge! Life is Huge! Life is Huge! Life is Huge! Life is Huge! Life is H
is Huge! Life is Huge! Life is Huge! Life is Huge! Life is Huge! Life is Huge! L
! Life is Huge! Life is Huge! Life is Huge! Life is Huge! Life is Huge! Life is H
is Huge! Life is Huge! Life is Huge! Life is Huge! Life is Huge! Life is Huge!
! Life is Huge! Life is Huge! Life is Huge! Life is Huge! Life is Huge! Life is H
is Huge! Life is Huge! Life is Huge! Life is Huge! Life is Huge! Life is Huge!
! Life is Huge! Life is Huge! Life is Huge! Life is Huge! Life is Huge! Life is H

STATEMENT OF INTENTION

I am grateful for the gift of life. I won't squander this wonderful gift. I commit to growing, exploring, expanding, participating and taking in the riches and opportunities that surround me every day of my life. Life is Huge! And I am privileged to be a part of it all.

Affirmation of the Day

With eyes of gratitude, I see the beauty around me.

I commit 100% to each area of my life.
I know that I count and I act as if I do.

MY LIFE IS RICH!

FAMILY

FRIENDS

HEALTH

PERSONAL GROWTH

SPIRITUAL GROWTH

ALONE TIME

RELATIONSHIP

CONTRIBUTION TO COMMUNITY

PLAYTIME

WORK

RISK OF THE DAY

TODAY I AM GRATEFUL FOR

Where do I belong today on my Pain-to-Power Chart?

▶ ▶

PAIN   **POWER**

I am grateful for the gift of life. I won't squander this wonderful gift. I commit to growing, exploring, expanding, participating and taking in the riches and opportunities that surround me every day of my life. Life is Huge! And I am privileged to be a part of it all.

Affirmation of the Day

I stop resisting and open up to exciting possibilities.

I commit 100% to each area of my life.
I know that I count and I act as if I do.

MY LIFE IS RICH!

FAMILY

FRIENDS

HEALTH

PERSONAL GROWTH

SPIRITUAL GROWTH

ALONE TIME

RELATIONSHIP

CONTRIBUTION TO COMMUNITY

PLAYTIME

WORK

RISK OF THE DAY

TODAY I AM GRATEFUL FOR

Where do I belong today on my Pain-to-Power Chart?

▶ ▶

PAIN   **POWER**

STATEMENT OF INTENTION

I am grateful for the gift of life. I won't squander this wonderful gift. I commit to growing, exploring, expanding, participating and taking in the riches and opportunities that surround me every day of my life. Life is Huge! And I am privileged to be a part of it all.

Affirmation of the Day

I let go of the struggle and dance with life.

I commit 100% to each area of my life.
I know that I count and I act as if I do.

MY LIFE IS RICH!

FAMILY

FRIENDS

HEALTH

PERSONAL GROWTH

SPIRITUAL GROWTH

ALONE TIME

RELATIONSHIP

CONTRIBUTION TO COMMUNITY

PLAYTIME

WORK

RISK OF THE DAY

TODAY I AM GRATEFUL FOR

Where do I belong today on my Pain-to-Power Chart?

▶ ▶

PAIN   **POWER**

STATEMENT OF INTENTION

am grateful for the gift of life. I won't squander this wonderful gift. I commit to growing, exploring, expanding, participating and taking in the riches and opportunities that surround me every day of my life. Life is Huge! And I am privileged to be a part of it all.

Affirmation of the Day

I embrace the 'ordinary' miracles of everyday life.

> I commit 100% to each area of my life.
> I know that I count and I act as if I do.

MY LIFE IS RICH!

FAMILY

FRIENDS

HEALTH

PERSONAL GROWTH

SPIRITUAL GROWTH

ALONE TIME

RELATIONSHIP

CONTRIBUTION TO COMMUNITY

PLAYTIME

WORK

RISK OF THE DAY

TODAY I AM GRATEFUL FOR

Where do I belong today on my Pain-to-Power Chart?

▶▶▶▶▶▶▶▶▶▶▶▶▶▶▶▶▶▶▶▶▶▶

PAIN   **POWER**

STATEMENT OF INTENTION

I am grateful for the gift of life. I won't squander this wonderful gift. I commit to growing, exploring, expanding, participating and taking in the riches and opportunities that surround me every day of my life. Life is Huge! And I am privileged to be a part of it all.

Affirmation of the Day

I am finding the gift in all that life brings me.

I commit 100% to each area of my life.
I know that I count and I act as if I do.

MY LIFE IS RICH!

FAMILY

FRIENDS

HEALTH

PERSONAL GROWTH

SPIRITUAL GROWTH

ALONE TIME

RELATIONSHIP

CONTRIBUTION TO COMMUNITY

PLAYTIME

WORK

RISK OF THE DAY

TODAY I AM GRATEFUL FOR

Where do I belong today on my Pain-to-Power Chart?

▶ ▶

PAIN   **POWER**

STATEMENT OF INTENTION

I am grateful for the gift of life. I won't squander this wonderful gift. I commit to growing, exploring, expanding, participating and taking in the riches and opportunities that surround me every day of my life. Life is Huge! And I am privileged to be a part of it all.

Affirmation of the Day

*I am patient and let life unfold in its own time
and in its own way.*

I commit 100% to each area of my life.
I know that I count and I act as if I do.

MY LIFE IS RICH!

FAMILY

FRIENDS

HEALTH

PERSONAL GROWTH

SPIRITUAL GROWTH

ALONE TIME

RELATIONSHIP

CONTRIBUTION TO COMMUNITY

PLAYTIME

WORK

RISK OF THE DAY

TODAY I AM GRATEFUL FOR

Where do I belong today on my Pain-to-Power Chart?

▶ ▶

PAIN   **POWER**

STATEMENT OF INTENTION

I am grateful for the gift of life. I won't squander this wonderful gift. I commit to growing, exploring, expanding, participating and taking in the riches and opportunities that surround me every day of my life. Life is Huge! And I am privileged to be a part of it all.

Affirmation of the Day

I learn something valuable from all life experiences.

> I commit 100% to each area of my life.
> I know that I count and I act as if I do.

MY LIFE IS RICH!

FAMILY

FRIENDS

HEALTH

PERSONAL GROWTH

SPIRITUAL GROWTH

ALONE TIME

RELATIONSHIP

CONTRIBUTION TO COMMUNITY

PLAYTIME

WORK

RISK OF THE DAY

TODAY I AM GRATEFUL FOR

Where do I belong today on my Pain-to-Power Chart?

▶ ▶ ▶ ▶ ▶ ▶ ▶ ▶ ▶ ▶ ▶ ▶ ▶ ▶ ▶ ▶ ▶ ▶ ▶ ▶

PAIN   **POWER**

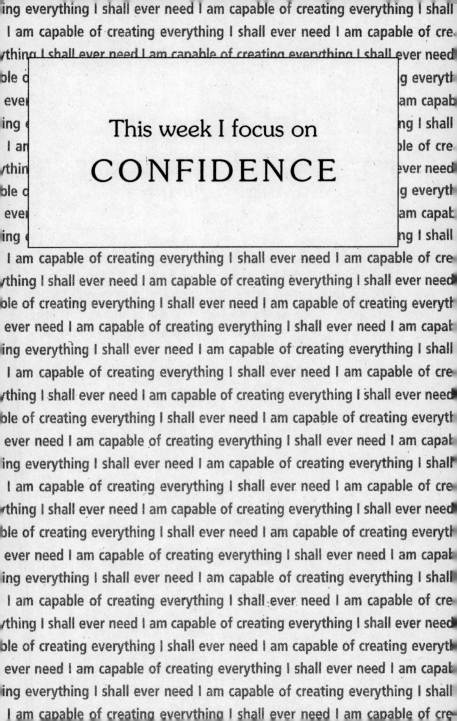

This week I focus on
CONFIDENCE

STATEMENT OF INTENTION

I feel the safety and caring that my soul radiates. I now claim my inner strength. I stand tall with the knowledge that 'I am a strong and loving human being'. I feel blessed to be a source of light and life. I move into life with energy and excitement. *Nothing* can stop me now!

Affirmation of the Day

I am capable of creating everything I shall ever need.

> I commit 100% to each area of my life.
> I know that I count and I act as if I do.

MY LIFE IS RICH!

FAMILY

FRIENDS

HEALTH

PERSONAL GROWTH

SPIRITUAL GROWTH

ALONE TIME

RELATIONSHIP

CONTRIBUTION TO COMMUNITY

PLAYTIME

WORK

RISK OF THE DAY

TODAY I AM GRATEFUL FOR

Where do I belong today on my Pain-to-Power Chart?

▶ ▶

PAIN   **POWER**

feel the safety and caring that my soul radiates. I now claim my inner strength. I stand tall with the knowledge that 'I am a strong and loving human being'. I feel blessed to be a source of light and life. I move into life with energy and excitement. *Nothing* can stop me now!

Affirmation of the Day

The quality of my life depends only on me.

> I commit 100% to each area of my life.
> I know that I count and I act as if I do.

MY LIFE IS RICH!

FAMILY

FRIENDS

HEALTH

PERSONAL GROWTH

SPIRITUAL GROWTH

ALONE TIME

RELATIONSHIP

CONTRIBUTION TO COMMUNITY

PLAYTIME

WORK

RISK OF THE DAY

TODAY I AM GRATEFUL FOR

Where do I belong today on my Pain-to-Power Chart?

▶ ▶ ▶ ▶ ▶ ▶ ▶ ▶ ▶ ▶ ▶ ▶ ▶ ▶ ▶ ▶ ▶ ▶ ▶ ▶

PAIN   **POWER**

STATEMENT OF INTENTION

feel the safety and caring that my soul radiates. I now claim my inner strength. I stand tall with the knowledge that 'I am a strong and loving human being'. I feel blessed to be a source of light and life. I move into life with energy and excitement. *Nothing* can stop me now!

Affirmation of the Day

I am finding a solution to all tasks set before me.

I commit 100% to each area of my life.
I know that I count and I act as if I do.

MY LIFE IS RICH!

FAMILY

FRIENDS

HEALTH

PERSONAL GROWTH

SPIRITUAL GROWTH

ALONE TIME

RELATIONSHIP

CONTRIBUTION TO COMMUNITY

PLAYTIME

WORK

RISK OF THE DAY

TODAY I AM GRATEFUL FOR

Where do I belong today on my Pain-to-Power Chart?

▶ ▶

PAIN   **POWER**

STATEMENT OF INTENTION

I feel the safety and caring that my soul radiates. I now claim my inner strength. I stand tall with the knowledge that 'I am a strong and loving human being'. I feel blessed to be a source of light and life. I move into life with energy and excitement. *Nothing* can stop me now!

Affirmation of the Day

I am on the path to the best of who I am.

I commit 100% to each area of my life.
I know that I count and I act as if I do.

MY LIFE IS RICH!

FAMILY

FRIENDS

HEALTH

PERSONAL GROWTH

SPIRITUAL GROWTH

ALONE TIME

RELATIONSHIP

CONTRIBUTION TO COMMUNITY

PLAYTIME

WORK

RISK OF THE DAY

TODAY I AM GRATEFUL FOR

Where do I belong today on my Pain-to-Power Chart?

▶ ▶

PAIN   **POWER**

STATEMENT OF INTENTION

I feel the safety and caring that my soul radiates. I now claim my inner strength. I stand tall with the knowledge that 'I am a strong and loving human being'. I feel blessed to be a source of light and life. I move into life with energy and excitement. *Nothing* can stop me now!

Affirmation of the Day

I release my fear about the outcome of all situations in my life.

> I commit 100% to each area of my life.
> I know that I count and I act as if I do.

MY LIFE IS RICH!

FAMILY

FRIENDS

HEALTH

PERSONAL GROWTH

SPIRITUAL GROWTH

ALONE TIME

RELATIONSHIP

CONTRIBUTION TO COMMUNITY

PLAYTIME

WORK

RISK OF THE DAY

TODAY I AM GRATEFUL FOR

Where do I belong today on my Pain-to-Power Chart?

▶ ▶

PAIN   **POWER**

STATEMENT OF INTENTION

I feel the safety and caring that my soul radiates. I now claim my inner strength. I stand tall with the knowledge that 'I am a strong and loving human being'. I feel blessed to be a source of light and life. I move into life with energy and excitement. *Nothing* can stop me now!

Affirmation of the Day

Today ... and every day, I embrace the world like a lover!

> I commit 100% to each area of my life.
> I know that I count and I act as if I do.

MY LIFE IS RICH!

FAMILY

FRIENDS

HEALTH

PERSONAL GROWTH

SPIRITUAL GROWTH

ALONE TIME

RELATIONSHIP

CONTRIBUTION TO COMMUNITY

PLAYTIME

WORK

RISK OF THE DAY

TODAY I AM GRATEFUL FOR

Where do I belong today on my Pain-to-Power Chart?

▶ ▶

PAIN   **POWER**